INDESTRUCTIBLE
joy

for the Next Generations

EDITED BY
DAVID AND SALLY MICHAEL

Truth:78

PRODUCTION:
Managing Editor: Candice Watters
Designer: Laura Johns
Editorial Review: Jill Nelson and Karen Hieb

*Equipping the Next Generations to
Know, Honor, and Treasure God*

Truth78.org
info@Truth78.org
877.400.1414
@Truth78org

To John Piper—

WHO NOT ONLY GAVE us the phrase "Indestructible Joy," but has also devoted his life to helping us, and the rest of the world, see and savor this joy in a God who is most glorified in us when we are most satisfied in Him through Jesus Christ.

In the early 1980s, our eyes were opened to see a God many of us had never seen before—a God who was infinitely more glorious than we ever realized. We wondered how we could grow up going to Sunday school and be nearly 30 years old before seeing God in this way. We resolved that it would be different for the generations coming behind us, and thus Children Desiring God, now Truth78, was born.

John, the fingerprints of your Bible-saturated teaching are all over this ministry. We will forever rejoice in this God who gave you to us for His glory and for the indestructible joy of His people to all generations.

Give ear, O my people, to my teaching;
   incline your ears to the words of my mouth!
I will open my mouth in a parable;
   I will utter dark sayings from of old,
things that we have heard and known,
   that our fathers have told us.
We will not hide them from their children,
   but tell to the coming generation
the glorious deeds of the LORD, and his might,
   and the wonders that he has done.

He established a testimony in Jacob
   and appointed a law in Israel,
which he commanded our fathers
   to teach to their children,
that the next generation might know them,
   the children yet unborn,
and arise and tell them to their children,
   so that they should set their hope in God
and not forget the works of God,
   but keep his commandments;
and that they should not be like their fathers,
   a stubborn and rebellious generation,
a generation whose heart was not steadfast,
   whose spirit was not faithful to God.

PSALM 78:1-8

Contents

INDESTRUCTIBLE JOY
for the next generations

Introduction

For the Indestructible Joy
of the Next Generations

AS A CONCLUSION to his famous Sermon on the Mount, Jesus told a story that, for generations, has been famous among Sunday school children and, for decades, has captured the desire of our hearts for the next generations:

> "Everyone then who hears these words of mine and does them will be like a wise man who built his house on the rock. And the rain fell, and the floods came, and the winds blew and beat on that house, but it did not fall, because it had been founded on the rock. And everyone who hears these words of mine and does not do them will be like a foolish man who built his house on the sand. And the rain fell, and the floods came, and the winds blew and beat against that house, and it fell, and great was the fall of it" (Matthew 7:24-27).

We don't want to raise a generation of fools who grow up hearing, yet neglecting, the words of Jesus. We want our children to be among the wise in their generation. We want them to be equipped for living by faith in the Son of God, walking in His ways, trusting Him in every circumstance, standing firm against the schemes of the devil, forsaking the things of this world and the desires of the flesh, laying up treasures in heaven, holding fast with confidence in His goodness, resting in His sovereignty, running with endurance the race that is set before them, persevering in the full assurance of hope, pressing on toward the goal for the prize of the upward call of God in Christ Jesus, standing on the promises of God, and enduring in an unshakable faith when the inevitable storms of life blow and beat against them. The fruit of this unshakable faith is an indestructible joy.

As Jesus' final hour was approaching he warned his disciples that the storms were coming. "Then they will deliver you up to tribulation and put you to death, and you will be hated by all nations for my name's sake" (Matthew 24:9). On the night before He endured the cross, Jesus said, "Truly, truly...you will weep and lament, but the world will rejoice. You will be sorrowful..." But on the heels of that warning, Jesus quickly assured them that their "'sorrow will turn into joy....and no one will take your joy from you" (John 16:20-22). In other words, the fruit of their unshakable faith was an indestructible joy.

For more than 20 years, the pursuit of this indestructible joy for the next generations has been the heartbeat of Children Desiring God. On several occasions during this span, God used many voices to inspire, encourage, and support thousands in this pursuit as men and women from across this country and around the world gathered in Minnesota, and once in Indiana, for our national conferences. This book is an effort to gather a taste of these timeless messages into one place with the prayer that they will continue to inspire, encourage, and support thousands more. As you read the words of these servants, and perhaps listen to their original messages online at **Truth78.org/anthology,** let them serve as a reminder of this pursuit that has defined our ministry. This pursuit for indestructible joy remains unchanged as Children Desiring God begins this new season as Truth78.

1

No Greater Joy

*Leading the next generations
to walk in the truth*

DAVID MICHAEL

IN A MESSAGE on Romans 7:2-10, Mark Vroegop, pastor of College Park Church, gave a helpful illustration of the Christian life.[1] The image was of a long escalator clicking its way downward away from Christ and toward destruction. The escalator is crowded with masses of people being carried away by the downward pull in the culture of unbelief. The crowd is blissfully unaware or unconcerned about the everlasting torment that awaits them at the bottom.

At the top of the escalator is Christ, and with Him everlasting joy. There is no up-escalator for the Christian who is seeking Christ. We cannot coast our way into joy. When we become a Christian, by God's grace, we turn around on the down-escalator and strive against the gravitational pull of the world and of our own sinful flesh. We turn and pursue Christ, who for the joy that was set before Him (at the top of the escalator) endured the cross and bore the shame and all

---

[1] Mark Vroegop, "Is the Law Bad, Good, or What?" Sermon preached at College Park Church. Indianapolis, IN. November 16, 2014. http://www.yourchurch.com/sermon/is-the-law-bad-or-good-or-what/

the gravitational forces against Him (Hebrews 12:2).

The Christian life is following Jesus up the down-escalator, "press[ing] on toward the goal for the prize of the upward call of God in Christ Jesus" (Philippians 3:14). This is an illustration of the Christian life and an illustration of our vision for the next generation.

Our earnest desire and prayer is that, by the grace of God, our children will turn and fix their opened eyes on the beauty of the One who goes before them. As they mature, we want our children to be well-equipped to walk in the way that the Lord has set before them. For the sake of Christ, we want to effectively and winsomely engage with the Gospel those who are going the other way. We want them saturated with the Word of God and with the sword of the Spirit in their hand, fighting the fight of faith, enduring all the dangers, toils, and snares along the way. We want them persevering in faithfulness to their last breath. When they meet their Savior, we want them to be looking into a radiant face as the Master says, "well done, good, faithful, persevering servant—enter into the JOY of your master" (Matthew 25:21).

Our vision for the next generation is a vision for the indestructible joy of our children, and for the unsurpassable joy of those who love them and care about the outcome of their faith. 3 John 1-8 says,

> The elder to the beloved Gaius, whom I love in truth. Beloved, I pray that all may go well with you and that you may be in good health, as it goes well with your soul. For I rejoiced greatly when the brothers came and testified to your truth, as indeed you are walking in the truth. I have no greater joy than to hear that my children are walking in the truth. Beloved, it is a faithful thing you do in all your efforts for these brothers, strangers as they are, who testified to your love before the church. You will do well to send them on their journey in a manner worthy of God. For they have gone out for the sake of the name, accepting nothing from the Gentiles. Therefore we ought to support people like these, that we may be fellow workers for the truth (3 John 1-8).

My prayer is that we will be able to join with the apostle and say, "I have no greater joy than to hear that my children are walking in the truth."

Consider the situation that prompted the apostle to make this amazing claim. By the time John wrote this letter, it had been many years since he and his brother James left their nets and followed Jesus. John was probably in his 80s when he wrote this letter to Gaius, whom he knew and loved like a son.

John's aim in this short letter is to address a problem caused by Diotrephes, who was one of the leaders in the church. Diotrephes not only refused to welcome some traveling missionaries that John commended to the church, but he was also expelling those who showed hospitality to them.

As unhappy as he was with Diotrephes' behavior, John was very glad to hear that Gaius had welcomed these strangers, treated them as brothers in the Lord, and extended hospitality and care to them—"For I rejoiced greatly when the brothers came and testified to your truth, as indeed you are walking in the truth" (v. 3).

To say that he "rejoiced greatly" is saying a lot, but it is even more to say he has *"no greater joy..."* (v. 4). It is worth taking some time to consider why John can make such a claim. But before we do, it should be noted that when John speaks of "his children," he is not referring to children growing up in his immediate family. Throughout John's letters he often addresses the people he is writing to as his "children," and even his "little children." In these instances he is speaking of those who have come to faith through his preaching and teaching ministry. These are what we might call his "spiritual children."

I am eager for parents, grandparents, and all who are involved in the lives of children to be encouraged by John's testimony in this passage and to experience his joy. This unsurpassable joy should be our response when we hear or observe that anyone—young or old—related or not—is walking in the truth. May God grant us every grace we need to faithfully pursue this joy for the sake of the next generations.

Let's now consider four reasons why John could make the extraordinary claim that there is no greater joy than the joy of hearing that our children are walking in the truth.

JOHN TREASURED THE TRUTH HIMSELF

By this time, John had devoted most of his life to proclaiming the truth that Gaius was walking in. Nothing gave John more joy, than witnessing people embrace this truth and then begin walking in it. He expressed this joy in his second letter when he wrote, "I rejoiced greatly to find some of your children walking in the truth..." (2 John 1:4). In fact, John begins that letter by referring to himself as "the elder" to the church, which he refers to as "the elect lady and her children, whom I love in truth, and not only I, but also all who know the truth because of the truth that abides in us and will be with us forever" (2 John 1:1-2). The reason John experienced this extraordinary joy when he witnessed others walking in the truth is that he treasured the truth himself. It follows then, that treasuring the truth ourselves is the first step toward experiencing the extraordinary joy of knowing that our children are walking in the truth.

JOHN FEARED GOD

A second reason why John was so delighted to hear of Gaius' faithfulness was because he knew what was at stake if this spiritual child of his did not walk in the truth. John understood that if Gaius had not been walking toward everlasting joy in the light of truth, he would be walking toward everlasting sorrow in the darkness of unbelief. John understood that there are only two possible eternal outcomes for our children. The thought of our children eternally separated from Christ in hell should make us tremble. In pondering the horrors of hell, we are more likely to magnify our joy when our children forsake their self-destructive trajectory and set their course toward the everlasting joys of heaven with Christ.

JOHN WITNESSED THE FRUIT OF HIS LABOR

For believers who love the truth there is joy whenever we hear of someone walking in it, whether we know them or not. Our hearts can sing for joy when we hear a testimony of how God brought someone out of darkness and into the light. However, if you happen to be the person God used to bring that soul to faith; and if you showed the wanderer his way; and if you labored and devoted your life to showing new believers how to walk in the Truth; and if you poured out your heart and soul in prayer for them—then when the day comes when they start walking—your heart will leap with joy and will rejoice with John in saying, "I have no greater joy than that!"

GAIUS WAS *WALKING* IN THE TRUTH

There would be no joy if all Gaius did was give lip service to the truth. Certainly John was happy that Gaius *knew the truth* because John knew how important it is to know the truth. Knowing the truth precedes walking in it. We must be devoted to imparting the truth to our children. But knowing and understanding the truth is of little use unless we are walking in it.

In his first letter, John wrote these words:

> This is the message we have heard from him and proclaim to you, that God is light, and in him is no darkness at all. If we say we have fellowship with him while we walk in darkness, we lie and do not practice the truth [we do not walk in the truth] (1 John 1:5-6).

There are many people who have grown up in Christian homes and have heard the truth all their lives. They will even tell you that they have fellowship with Christ. They will say they know Jesus and are following Him, but they have never changed direction. They are still coasting their way to destruction.

Diotrephes likely knew the truth. He was a leader in the church, but according to John, he was self-centered, rebellious, arrogant, and wicked. In 3 John 9, we learn that he "likes to put himself first" and "does not acknowledge our [John's] authority," and in verse 10, John says that he was "talking wicked nonsense against us." Diotrephes was clearly *not* walking in the truth. Not only did he fail to extend hospitality to these visitors, but also he was ousting from the church those who were being hospitable to them.

By contrast, Gaius *knew* the truth and believed the truth, and it showed in the way he lived. It was not just head knowledge for him. When these visiting brothers came, he knew the Christ-honoring way to treat them and, unlike Diotrephes, he did it. He welcomed these brothers by extending grace and hospitality to them. You can almost sense John saying: "Way to go Gaius!!! You knew the right thing to do and you did it!"

Truth78 is committed to serving the local church by inspiring and encouraging the pursuit of this indestructible joy for the sake of the next generations. There are three priorities that we believe should shape the ministries of the church for children and youth:

A SERIOUS COMMITMENT TO IMPARTING TRUTH TO THE NEXT GENERATIONS

In his book, *Transforming Children into Spiritual Champions*, George Barna lays out his findings based on his extensive research regarding children and faith. Barna challenges the church and parents to consciously raise children with a biblical worldview, identifying four cornerstones that are necessary:

1. **THE BIBLE'S AUTHORITY**—belief that the Bible is the only trustworthy source of wisdom and truth for life, rather than looking to other sources for wisdom; or considering the Bible to be one of several truth claims, rather than the one and only truth claim.

2. **THE BIBLE'S CONTENT**—rather than a shallow grasp of select Bibles stories, characters, and a few verses.

3. **THE BIBLE'S FRAMEWORK**—to help young people connect the dots of God's principles so that they draw a striking picture of truth and purpose, rather than failing to tie Bible teaching into a logical and comprehensive framework that makes sense and provides practical counsel.

4. **THE DESIRE TO OBEY GOD**—ultimately, the Spirit of God must burn that desire into their hearts, but we dare not passively wait for that to happen. In Deuteronomy 6:5-7, the Lord says: "You shall love the LORD your God with all your heart and with all your soul and with all your might. And these words that I command you today shall be on

your heart...teach them diligently to your children..."
Without this burning desire our children will not
walk in the Truth.²

The Lord makes it clear that faithful instruction of children in the truth begins with us: parents, pastors, and teachers. We must first love the Lord our God with all our hearts if we desire our children to have the same affection for the Lord. The Lord's Words must first be on our hearts before we can "teach them diligently to [our] children." It is important that we know the truth, and even more important that we have a whole-hearted love for it. In other words, if we want our children to walk in the truth, it is important that they walk with people who are walking in the truth. This takes us to the second priority.

THE STRATEGIC SUPPORT, ENCOURAGEMENT, AND EQUIPPING OF PARENTS

The people who have the most access, the best opportunity, and the greatest potential influence—not to mention the biblical responsibility for helping children walk in the truth—are their parents. Our plea to parents and grandparents is that they make the most of the fleeting opportunity they have.

The life of a parent today can quickly become consumed by so many good things that there is little time left for what is most important. Parents must not trade the greater things for lesser things.

- What will it profit a child to be an accomplished pianist but spend his life as a fool?
- What will it benefit a child to have all the friends in the world—even good Christian friends—but have no friend in Jesus on Judgment day?
- What good will it do for a child to marry well but never sit at the marriage feast of the lamb?

---

² George Barna, *Transforming Children into Spiritual Champions* (Grand Rapids, MI: Baker Books, 2003), 67-69.

- What benefit will there be for the child who makes it to the national championship on his way to destruction?
- What will it profit a child to gain the whole world and lose his soul? (Mark 8:36)

Imparting the truth to our children is essential and should be the primary focus for the church's ministries to children and youth. However, the best two hours of children's programming is no substitute for the passionate and intentional pursuit by parents of everlasting joy for their children. The church is best equipped to encourage, support, challenge, and develop resources for parents in their work of discipling their children.

Barna asked the churches in his study how they measured success in their ministry to children and youth. Most, he said, pointed to "growing numbers of students enrolled, consistent attendance, completion of curriculum in the allotted time, parental satisfaction, minimal discipline problems, etc."[3] However, the most effective churches, Barna observed, identified three very different indicators of success. In summary:

- Involvement of parents in the spiritual development of their children. The effort to nurture children is deemed deficient if it is not led by the parents themselves, in close partnership with the church.
- Strategic equipping of parents to help children develop spiritually. Parents are not naturally skilled at discipling their children. They need the input and training that churches are uniquely called to supply.
- Tangible evidence of transformation in children's lives. Parroting Sunday school facts falls short of the lifestyle changes that testify to a deeper renovation of the heart and spirit.[4]

THE PRIORITY OF PRAYER

As much as we may desire that our children walk in the truth, and as much as we might encourage them to that end, we cannot

---

[3]   Barna, 109.
[4]   Barna, 110.

make them walk in the truth. We can teach them the truth. We can commend the truth to them. But we cannot make them love the truth. We cannot orient their lives and their affections to the truth. We are powerless over the hearts of our children. The good news is that the God who made your children holds their heart in His hand.

Proverbs 21:1 tell us that "the king's heart is a stream of water in the hand of the LORD; he turns it wherever he will." In 1 Corinthians 3:6-7, Paul says, "I planted, Apollos watered, but God gave the growth. So neither he who plants nor he who waters is anything, but only God who gives the growth." Psalm 127:1 says, "Unless the LORD builds the house, those who build it labor in vain. Unless the LORD watches over the city, the watchman stays awake in vain."

Since we have no power over the hearts of our children and since we unable to give them what matters most, then prayer to the One who can turn the heart around is an indispensable step that leads us to insurmountable joy.

According to Barna, the churches with the most effective and fruitful ministries to children were serious about prayer. He said, "the prayer investment made by the effective churches may be the single most important venture of their ministries."[5] He found the most productive children's ministries have five areas of prayer focus. In summary, they are:

1. Teachers praying for each of their students on a regular basis.

2. Teachers praying as a team, usually on a weekly basis, along with other staff and church leaders in the children's ministry.

3. Intercessors volunteering to faithfully pray for the teachers and students.

---

[5] Barna, 102.

4. The entire congregation frequently praying for children's ministry, and

5. Parents praying during prayer times organized by the church, and in connection with prayer partners.[6]

A WORD TO THOSE WHO CARRY A "LIVING CROSS"

As we consider the great joy that we have when we hear that our children are walking in the truth, I am painfully aware of the great sorrow we endure when our children forsake the truth and continue to walk in darkness. In 1873, while preaching on 3 John 4, Charles Spurgeon said:

> No cross is so heavy to carry as a living cross. Next to a woman who is bound to an ungodly husband or a man who is unequally yoked with a graceless wife, I pity the father whose children are not walking in the truth, who yet is himself an earnest Christian. Must it always be so, that the father shall go to the house of God and his son to the alehouse? Shall the father sing the songs of Zion, and the son and daughter pour forth the ballads of Belial? Must we come to the communion table alone, and our children be separated from us? Must we go on the road to holiness and the way of peace, and behold our dearest ones traveling with the multitude the broad way, despising what we prize, rebelling against Him who we adore? God grant it may not be so...[7]

I want to conclude by offering some words of hope to those who are carrying this "living cross" and who, with the Apostle Paul, say, "I have great sorrow and unceasing anguish in my heart. For I could wish that I myself were accursed and cut off from Christ for the sake of my brothers, my kinsmen [my children] according to the flesh" (Romans 9:2-3).

---

6 Barna, 102-104.
7 Charles Spurgeon, "A Parent's and Pastor's Joy." Sermon preached December 21, 1873. *Spurgeon's Sermons on Family and Home* (Grand Rapids, MI: Kregel Publications, 1995), 28.

BEWARE OF THE ACCUSER OF THE BRETHREN (REVELATION 12:10)

We have an ancient foe who is a liar and a murderer from the beginning. So often when we emphasize the important role that parents play in the spiritual development of their children and challenge them to be vigilant and faithful to their God-given call, some parents feel judged. They assume that if their children are not walking in the truth, they must have done something wrong and then condemn themselves.

We must be careful not to believe the lie. The unbelief of a child is not punishment for parental failure. Many parents of unbelieving children have been faithful and should not listen to the accuser. Perhaps a parent can look back and remember times when he sinned against his child. If this is the case, he should confess his sin, look to the cross where that sin was covered, and ask for forgiveness while trusting the living God who accomplishes His purposes regardless of his sin.

If our weakness as parents is exposed by something we should have done differently, then we should boast with the Apostle Paul in that weakness, while trusting the One whose power is made perfect in it (2 Corinthians 12:9). Mercifully, our imperfection as parents cannot restrain the hand of God. He always accomplishes His purpose (Isaiah 46:10).

SURRENDER ALL WORLDLY CLAIM UPON THEIR LIVES IN HOPE

When Sally and I dedicated our daughters to the Lord, one of the promises we made was that we would "surrender all worldly claim upon their lives in the hope that they would belong wholly to God forever." According to Psalm 127:3, our children are given to us by God. However, even though He has given them to us, they still belong to Him. You might say that God "retains the title" for our children. He retains sovereign rights to lead them where He will, and work in them everything that is pleasing in His sight. We surrender to Him any claim to the ownership of our children in the hope that they will belong wholly to God forever. We trust Him to call them to Himself on His terms and on His timetable.

Rather than giving in to fear, discouragement, hopelessness, or anger, it is helpful for the parent carrying this "living cross" to consider this question: "If you knew that your child's disturbing behavior and foolishness was going to bring him to a saving encounter with the living Christ, would you feel differently?

We all want our children to have the benefit of growing up in a Christian home. We all want them to hear the truth and then embrace it and walk in it. We want them to have a relationship with the living Christ from a young age. Still, we have heard enough conversion stories to know that this is not always the way God brings the children of Christian parents to faith. Sometimes God will use the means that we fear the most. We must trust Him and yield our hearts to His way and the purpose He has for our children.

AS LONG AS THERE IS BREATH, THERE IS HOPE

We not only trust God's way, but we trust His timetable. It does not always make sense to us why God ordains that some people spend most of their lives coasting down the road to destruction. For 87 years, Ellen Olson persistently resisted anything having to do with Christianity and was dangerously close to the bottom of the "escalator" when the pursuing grace of God came upon her and transformed her into a passionate follower of Christ. God gave her a contagious affection for Jesus, and she will always be remembered as one of the most radiant Christians I have ever known. I don't know much about Ellen's mother except that she was a religious woman who made sure her daughter went to church. I have often wondered if her mom had prayed and shed tears over her Christ-forsaking daughter. If she did, she never tasted the 3 John 4 joy that we experienced as Ellen walked nine years in the truth, to her last breath.

BOW BEFORE THE SOVEREIGN HAND OF GOD

If the "King's heart is a stream of water in the hand of the LORD" (Proverbs 21:1), so also are the hearts of our children. Nothing is outside the power of God. Nothing can thwart His purposes—even the heart of the most rebellious child. We must never stop trusting the infinite wisdom and steadfast love, the enduring goodness and faithfulness of God.

Ultimately (and dreadfully) we must acknowledge and then put our hand over our mouths in humble submission to our God who has chosen some to be vessels of wrath (Romans 9:22). The thought of our children perishing in unbelief is a horrible thought, and we wonder how we could have joy in heaven knowing that our children are lost forever.

One Sunday morning of November 2002, Pastor John Piper was preaching on Romans 9:1-5 when he posed this question to us: "Will we then be sad throughout eternity because of those who are accursed and cut off from Christ in hell? Will heaven be a place of eternal grief? The answer is no."

He then quoted Jonathan Edwards, who answered that question like this: "With respect to any affection that the godly have had to the finally reprobate, the love of God will wholly swallow it up. And cause it wholly to cease."[8]

Pastor John continued,

Those who die in their sinful rebellion—we say it with tears now—will not have the power to hold heaven hostage with their own misery. Here we groan and weep. There we are consumed with the glory of Christ. Let [this] be a place where it is safe to grieve for wayward children. A place where parents who grieve find grace and support and not indictments.[9]

May God grant that our churches be safe places to grieve for wayward children. May they be places where grace and support can be found without indictment. And may they be places where the next generation is faithfully taught the full counsel of truth and witness the steadfast joy of all who hear that they are walking in the truth.

---

[8] Jonathan Edwards, *The Works of Jonathan Edwards* (Edinburgh: The Banner of Truth Trust), vol. 2, 899.

[9] John Piper, "Romans 9:1-5" (Sermon, Bethlehem church, Minneapolis, MN, November 10, 2002), https://www.desiringgod.org/messages/my-anguish-my-kinsmen-are-accursed

Gracious Father in heaven,

Together with my brothers and sisters who are reading these pages and for the sake of the children that they care about, we ask, in Jesus' name, that You lead these children out of darkness and into Your glorious light. We ask that You rescue them from the kingdom of Satan and make them citizens of Your unshakeable Kingdom. Turn them around and away from destruction and lead them to the everlasting joy of our Savior. If You must, let them be poor in this world but make them rich in faith and heirs of the Kingdom, which You have promised for all who love You.

Destroy all rivals to Your throne. Take away every god in their lives except God Almighty.

Take away from their affections, every treasure except the treasure of Jesus Christ their Savior. Neutralize the power of every spirit except the power of Your Holy Spirit working righteousness and peace within them. Bring every thought, every desire, every dream, every word, and every act under Your divine control. Overcome the deadly gravitational pull of their sin and turn them around that they might live and move and have their being in Christ, resting their hope and grounding their lives in Christ.

May not one of these children be lost, and one day soon, may those who love them and care for the outcome of their faith hear that these children are walking in the truth.

Make it so, dear Lord Jesus, for the glory of Your name and for our insurmountable joy.

Amen.

DAVID MICHAEL is co-founder of Truth78 and Pastor of Next Generation Ministries at College Park Church in Indianapolis, IN. He is married to Sally. They have two grown daughters and three grandchildren.

2

Declaring the Whole Counsel of God

What's at stake for our children

MARK VROEGOP

THE FIRST TIME I heard the Gospel clearly was from a children's worker. I don't remember her name, but I remember her clear presentation of the Gospel. Something within my heart burned. I knew what she was saying was true. I knew I was a sinner. I wanted to deal with my sin, and I was being drawn to Christ. After I arrived home, I went for a long walk in the woods. I was converted.

It is a great joy to think that there are thousands upon thousands of kids who will hear the Gospel because of Sunday school teachers and children's workers. They are the conduits of God's Word.

My wife teaches 50-75 children in our kindergarten Sunday school class. She loves platforming the Gospel for the hearts and lives of children. Faithful children's workers like her love teaching the Word and seeing the little lightbulbs turn on. They love seeing the beautiful things that happen in the context of children's lives. Their ministry shapes the hearts and minds of kids. But let's be honest. There are many times our children's workers are not really appreciated for all they do.

I'm convinced, however, that those who teach God's Word to children week after week are vital to mission of the church. They share a calling to teach the Word of God to the next generation with perseverance, completeness, and urgency. I'm grateful to God for them.

Their ministry is important culturally, theologically, morally, historically, biblically, and ecclesiologically.

- **CULTURALLY**—We are witnessing a worldview shift in our culture, a shift in values, and a shift in thinking.

- **THEOLOGICALLY**—Every person is a theologian. It isn't a matter of if you are a theologian. The question is whether or not you are a biblical one...and even children are theologians.

- **MORALLY**—Our children need to understand that from Genesis to Revelation there is a moral fabric that the Creator of the universe has kindly declared and imparted to us. This moral fabric is not something that we get to pick and choose.

- **HISTORICALLY**—Church history and biblical history are filled with examples of what happens when a generation grows up who "doesn't know the LORD" (Judges 2:10).

- **BIBLICALLY**—Children need to know and understand their Bible as a unified whole—not as marbles in a bowl, but as a string of pearls all linked together.

- **ECCLESIOLOGICALLY**—The very life of the church is at stake because of one reality: children grow up, and they become future leaders, elders, and members of our churches.

There are times I get discouraged when I look at the landscape of our culture and what my children and future grandchildren will face. And yet when I see faithful children's workers, it gives me some measure of hope, knowing that Sunday after Sunday there are teachers persevering in the whole counsel of God.

I want you to persevere in declaring the whole counsel of God because of what is at stake for our children. My aim is to show you how Paul approached his ministry, and to encourage you not to give up.

Acts 20 gives us a very personal glimpse into the ministry and heart of the Apostle Paul. After spending three years in Ephesus building up this strategic church, he is heading to Jerusalem amidst a very uncertain future. Before he departs, he calls the elders together.

Now from Miletus he sent to Ephesus and called the elders of the church to come to him. And when they came to him, he said to them:

"You yourselves know how I lived among you the whole time from the first day that I set foot in Asia, serving the Lord with all humility and with tears and with trials that happened to me through the plots of the Jews; how I did not shrink from declaring to you anything that was profitable, and teaching you in public and from house to house, testifying both to Jews and to Greeks of repentance toward God and of faith in our Lord Jesus Christ. And now, behold, I am going to Jerusalem, constrained by the Spirit, not knowing what will happen to me there, except that the Holy Spirit testifies to me in every city that imprisonment and afflictions await me. But I do not account my life of any value nor as precious to myself, if only I may finish my course and the ministry that I received from the Lord Jesus, to testify to the gospel of the grace of God. And now, behold, I know that none of you among whom I have gone about proclaiming the kingdom will see my face again. Therefore I testify to you this day that I am innocent of the blood of all, for I did not shrink from declaring to you the whole counsel of God. Pay careful attention to yourselves and to all the flock, in which the Holy Spirit has made you overseers, to care for the church of God, which he obtained with his own blood. I know that after my departure fierce wolves will come in among you, not sparing the flock; and from among your own selves will arise men speaking twisted things, to draw away the disciples after them. Therefore be alert, remembering that for three years I did not cease night or day to admonish everyone with tears. And now I commend you to God and to the Word of his grace, which is able to build you up and to give you the inheritance among all those who are sanctified" (Acts 20:17-32).

These are weighty words. His signature passage is this:

"Therefore I testify to you this day that I am innocent of the blood of all, for I did not shrink from declaring to you the whole counsel of God" (Acts 20:26-27).

These are the words of a pastor to his people, anticipating that they will be his final words. Ahead of Paul lies suffering, persecution, and probably death. These final moments are a crystallization of what ministry is really all about. You don't talk about secondary things when you think: "This is the last thing I am going to say."

What do we learn from Paul in these final words about church ministry? How does his message apply to ministry in the next generations? Let me suggest six ways:

1. PERSONALLY—IN A CONTEXT OF LIFE ON LIFE

And when they came to him, he said to them:

"You yourselves know how I lived among you the whole time from the first day that I set foot in Asia, serving the Lord with all humility and with tears and with trials that happened to me through the plots of the Jews;" (Acts 20:18-19)

Paul set his final words in the context of his time with them. According to Acts 20:31, it was a three-year ministry. It involved living among them, serving with humility, and suffering—with tears and trials. When Paul said he declared the whole counsel of God, he placed it in a vital context. This declaration was not just verbal; it was personal.

The content of what you teach is certainly imperative, but personal connection is central to the communication of God's Word. Your investment in the lives of children—your personal connection—provides the context for the Word of God to be received. The Word of

God was meant to be declared, but it was meant to be declared as you interact with someone in the context of his life.

For example, I had some great pastors in my life. However, I've been more deeply impacted by the sum total of a pastor's life, than by any single sermon. Your personal connection with the students to whom you minister is vital to the proclamation of the Gospel. The Ephesian elders were able to watch the life of the Apostle Paul.

The Word of God transmitted through the life of another person is not just a powerful tool for spiritual transformation, but it is actually the foundation of true, biblical ministry. Life on life is how the Word of God was meant to be heard.

2. SERIOUSLY—WITH A SENSE OF RESPONSIBILITY

In verse 26 Paul uses some strong language, "Therefore I testify to you this day that I am innocent of the blood of all of you." It sounds like Paul is making a courtroom statement. He uses language from Ezekiel 33 where the prophet is described as a watchman who has a moral responsibility to warn the people and deliver God's message. It says,

> "So you, son of man, I have made a watchman for the house of Israel. Whenever you hear a word from my mouth, you shall give them warning from me. If I say to the wicked, O wicked one, you shall surely die, and you do not speak to warn the wicked to turn from his way, that wicked person shall die in his iniquity, but his blood I will require at your hand. But if you warn the wicked to turn from his way, and he does not turn from his way, that person shall die in his iniquity, but you will have delivered your soul" (Ezekiel 33:7-9).

The prophet who warns and delivers God's message is innocent from the people's blood. But the prophet who fails to warn is culpable. As James 3:1 tells us, teachers will be judged with greater strictness. It is possible to teach in such a way that the teacher is guilty.

In Acts 18:6, Paul was opposed and reviled at Corinth by the Jews, and his response to the unbelieving Jews was, "Your blood be on your own heads! I am innocent." Paul had eternal life in mind here. By using blood, he is saying that his ministry was of such a character that he was innocent if any of them perished. He had declared to them the whole counsel of God. Paul could look at the elders from Ephesus and know that he was not guilty of their eternal destinies if any were lost. Paul had taught them what the Bible says. Therefore, he could say, "I am innocent."

Do you see the implications of this? There is a somber responsibility in the care of people's souls. A teacher can be guilty or innocent based upon how seriously the task is taken. I wonder how many parents, youth pastors, Sunday school teachers, pastors, and elder boards might be less than innocent because the people under their care are not being taught the full counsel of God. I wonder how many parents, youth pastors, children's workers, pastors, or elder councils have even thought about the question: "How do we declare the whole counsel of God?"

Ask yourself, "What is my role in teaching the whole counsel of God?" We must teach the Bible with a sense of responsibility.

3. FAITHFULLY—WITH COURAGEOUS CONSISTENCY

The next statement to consider is verse 27: "for I did not shrink from declaring to you the whole counsel of God." Paul believed that his ministry was characterized by teaching the Word in a way that was courageous and faithful. That statement, "I did not shrink" should sound familiar because he used it in verses 20-21, "I did not shrink from declaring to you anything that was profitable, and teaching you in public and from house to house...of faith in our Lord Jesus."

The words "shrink back" are translated "hesitate" in the NIV, which means to "hold back in uncertainty, unwillingness, or to avoid something."[1] Interestingly, in Hebrews 10:38, it is used for the person who fails to persevere by being faithless.

---

[1]   Johannes P. Louw and Eugene Albert Nida, *Greek-English Lexicon of the New Testament: Based on Semantic Domains* (New York, NY: United Bible Societies, 1996), 165.

"but my righteous one shall live by faith, and if he shrinks back, my soul has no pleasure in him." But we are not of those who shrink back and are destroyed, but of those who have faith and preserve their souls (Hebrews 10:38-39).

Shrinking back is the opposite of faith; it is unbelief.

In Acts 20, "to shrink from declaring the whole counsel of God" would mean succumbing to unbelief in the value of God's Word; to not have faith in God's Word, or particular aspects of God's Word—the whole counsel of God. Or to say it positively: to not shrink from declaring the whole counsel of God means that one believes that the entire message is valuable, important, and worthy.

Belief in the value of God's Word should result in faithfully teaching the Word—even particular aspects of God's Word that might be difficult. There are parts of the Bible that are tempting to "duck" or ignore. There are parts that are unsettling. There are sections that may disturb how you view the world, yourself, or others. Parts of the Bible demand radical obedience or sacrifice. But faith in the Bible requires faithful teachers who believe that it should be taught wisely, patiently, and courageously. To not shrink back means that we teach the whole Bible, not just the parts that people enjoy and like. (For more on teaching the difficult doctrines, see Chapter 5.)

The Bible assaults even a child's understanding of himself or herself. In my wife's class she teaches the Ten Commandments. It's remarkable that kindergartners do not believe they are sinners. They all know their brother or sister are sinners. "Oh, I'm good," they say, "but my brother is wicked!" The Bible corrects such warped self-awareness; it assaults the self-centeredness that is bound up in the heart of every human being, including the hearts of children. So it must be taught faithfully.

4. THOROUGHLY—WITH A UNIFIED, BALANCED, AND COMPREHENSIVE THEOLOGY

Now we come to the important phrase in verse 26, "the whole counsel of God." What created Paul's "blood innocence" in his teaching? What exactly is the whole counsel of God?

We can assume it doesn't mean Paul taught every verse in the Old Testament—line-by-line—with a full explanation. He didn't have time, and I do not believe that is the point. He is not saying, "I'm innocent because I taught you everything in the Old Testament." Instead, the whole counsel of God means the kind of biblical teaching that encompasses biblical Christianity in a unified, balanced, and comprehensive way. To teach the whole counsel of God's Word means that nothing important is left out.

Unified

To teach the whole counsel of God means comprehending the bigger-picture message of the Bible. Think of it like Jesus on the Emmaus road teaching two disciples, "And beginning with Moses and all the Prophets, he interpreted to them in all the Scriptures the things concerning himself" (Luke 24:27). Or consider the teaching of John:

> Now Jesus did many other signs in the presence of the disciples, which are not written in this book; but these are written so that you may believe that Jesus is the Christ, the Son of God, and that by believing you may have life in his name (John 20:30-31).

Unified means that the whole counsel of God connects the content of the Bible to the redemptive arc—the story of Creation-Fall-Redemption-Restoration. It is teaching in such a way that the plan of redemption is linked together. It involves uniting all the stories in the Bible to the greater story of the Gospel.

For example, the book of Exodus is not the story of Moses, nor the story of Israel, nor the story of Pharaoh. The book of Exodus is the story of God! In fact, God told Pharaoh that explicitly in Exodus 9:16, "But for this purpose I have raised you up, to show you my power, so that my name may be proclaimed in all the earth." Moses, Israel, and Pharaoh are simply the platform on which God says, "Look at my majesty and my glory." Throughout Israel's history, God keeps going back to the Exodus because it was the moment when He made it very clear that they were His people and all the gods of the nations of the earth are no match for the God of Abraham, Isaac, and Jacob.

Balanced

Teaching the whole counsel of God's Word requires helping people, including children, know what is most important. D.A. Carson says,

> What he [Paul] must mean is that he taught the burden of the whole of God's revelation, the balance of things, leaving nothing out that was of primary importance, never ducking the hard bits, helping believers to grasp the whole counsel of God...[2]

Balanced teaching means you teach the "and" of the Bible—that God is just and merciful; that God is full of wrath and full of love; that Jesus is fully God and fully man; that God is sovereign and man is responsible; that sin is serious and can be forgiven; that we are united with Christ and we still struggle with indwelling sin. The whole counsel of God highlights the "and" of balanced teaching.

Comprehensive

Teaching the whole counsel of God demands wrestling with big picture questions that span the length of the canon: Who created the universe? What does it mean to be an image-bearer? What happened when Adam and Eve sinned? Why did God choose Israel? What was the purpose of the Law, the sacrifices, and the tabernacle? Why did Jesus come into the world? Why did Jesus live and die and rise again? What is the church? Why was the Holy Spirit sent? How is a person saved? What does it mean to be obedient? How do we fight against sin? What is union with Christ? What is election, justification, sanctification, and glorification? What is God's vision for the nations? What will happen in the last days?

Oh to have a people who know the answers to those questions! Oh to have a people who love the glory of God, know the answers to those questions, and go out into a world that does not know the answers to those questions. Teaching the whole counsel of God answers basic questions like: Who is God? Who are we? What should I do? Where is hope?

---

[2] D. A. Carson, "Challenges for the Twenty-first-century Pulpit," in *Preach the Word: Essays on Expository Preaching: In Honor of R. Kent Hughes*, eds. Leland Ryken and Todd Wilson (Wheaton, IL: Crossway, 2007), 177-178.

One of the reasons catechisms were developed in the sixteenth and 17th centuries was to provide a way for the systematic teaching of the Bible. The Protestant Reformation featured the development of catechisms by Luther and Calvin, as well as the Heidelberg and Westminster Catechisms. Charles Spurgeon said,

> I am persuaded that the use of a good Catechism in all our families will be a great safeguard against the increasing errors of the times, and therefore I have compiled this little manual from the Westminster Assembly's and Baptist Catechisms, for the use of my own church and congregation. Those who use it in their families or classes must labor to explain the sense; but the words should be carefully learned by heart, for they will be understood better as years pass. May the Lord bless my dear friends and their families evermore...[3]

5. URGENTLY—KNOWING THE DANGERS AROUND US AND IN US

In verses 28 and 31 Paul urged them to be watchful:

> Pay careful attention to yourselves and to all the flock, in which the Holy Spirit has made you overseers, to care for the church of God, which he obtained with his own blood....Therefore be alert, remembering that for three years I did not cease night or day to admonish everyone with tears.

Paul knew there were dangers around them, and even within them. He urged them to be on guard because they were not in neutral territory. The whole counsel of God is not taught in a vacuum or isolation. It is set in the midst of a culture and context fraught with spiritual dangers. This was as true in Paul's day as it is in ours. The care of souls is serious and dangerous work.

Paul was concerned—even confident—that fierce wolves in the form of false teachers would come into the church and create havoc (v.

---

[3]   Charles Haddon Spurgeon, *A Puritan Catechism* (Legacy Publications via CreateSpace: Scotts Valley, CA, 2011), 1.

29). What's more, the false teachers would spring up from within their own ranks. Paul had personally experienced opposition from outside the church and from inside as well. He faced the kind of opposition and doctrinal error that crept into many churches. False teachers emerged and took over entire households. He encountered legalism, mysticism, Gnosticism, licentiousness, divisions, and spiritual warfare.

Paul knew the wicked capability of the human heart. He knew the devices of the enemy. This made teaching the whole counsel of God all the more important. His consistent pastoral strategy was to clearly teach the Word of God so that when some brand of false teaching emerged, it would be recognized.

I'm sure I don't need to convince you that we live in challenging cultural times. We are in the midst of a massive shift of values, ethics, and beliefs, which are a product of a generation of children who have been steeped in a post-modern mindset. We are reaping the spiritual fruit of the first generation that has been consistently told that there is no absolute truth, tolerance equals the allowance for any belief, morality is a matter of a chosen social construct, sexuality is a fluid category of ethics, and discovering who you are means not letting anyone or anything hold you back.

Contrast this with the first three questions of the Spurgeon catechism:

Q. What is the chief end of man?
A. *Man's chief end is to glorify God (1 Corinthians 10:31), and to enjoy Him forever (Psalm 73:25-26).*

Q. What rule has God given to direct us how we may glorify and enjoy Him?
A. *The Word of God which is contained in the Scriptures of the Old and New Testaments (Ephesians 2:20; 2 Timothy 3:16) is the only rule to direct us how we may glorify God and enjoy Him (1 John 1:3).*

Q. What do the Scriptures principally teach?
A. *The Scriptures principally teach what man is to*

*believe concerning God, and what duty God requires
of man (2 Timothy 1:13; Ecclesiastes 12:13).*[4]

Those who teach God's Word week in and week out are a beachhead of biblical truth. They may be the one voice imparting biblical truth into a child's mind or a teenager's heart. They must not give up. But this applies beyond teachers to the home. Let us not forget that dads and moms are a weighty voice in their children's hearts. They have a bigger pulpit than pastors, and they can impart biblical truth, or they can undo it.

There are spiritual, moral, and philosophical dangers around us and inside us. We need to realize that declaring the whole counsel of God needs to be pursued urgently because the voices and inputs from our culture are getting louder, more frequent, and more hostile to Christianity.

6. CONFIDENTLY—WITH ASSURANCE OF GOD'S GRACE AND HIS WORD

We conclude on a positive and encouraging note from verse 32,

And now I commend you to God and to the word of his grace, which is able to build you up and to give you the inheritance among all those who are sanctified.

Paul does not believe he is going to see these elders again, so what does he put his confidence in? In the Word of God's grace that is able to "build them up" and "give them an inheritance among the sanctified." He knows that the Word will give the people life and help them to persevere all the way to the end. He has taught them the whole counsel of God, he is innocent of their blood, and he commends them to God and to the Word of His grace.

Despite the threats, the challenges, and the potential problems, Paul lives confidently in God's plans for his life and the lives of the elders. He believes the sustaining grace of God will be mediated

---

[4]   Spurgeon, 2.

through the Word. As Paul leaves the Ephesian elders he knows they are in good care—God is sovereign, and the Word of God is central to their lives. Against the possibility of opposition, the threat of arrest, and his potential death, he is confident in God's plan and in the sustaining power of the Word.

Do you want the little hearts you teach every Sunday to persevere? Do you want them to hold on to Christ all their lives? Do you know the only guarantee for that? It is the grace of God and the Word of God. Our children must know the whole counsel of God's Word. We should strive for the goal of children growing into adults who lie on their death bed and say, "I believe in Jesus!"

I want you to have the same assurance Paul had—to know that you are working in cooperation with God's plan; knowing that His Word is able to build up the next generation. Be assured that faithfully teaching the Word—the whole counsel of God—is the means by which children endure all the way to end.

Acts 20 provides a compelling model for teaching the Scriptures. With so much at stake for our children, we must teach the Bible personally, seriously, faithfully, thoroughly, urgently, and confidently. The life-giving power of the whole counsel of God is our greatest hope for the next generation.

MARK VROEGOP is Lead Pastor of College Park Church in Indianapolis, IN. Mark and his wife, Sarah, have four children and one daughter who is in heaven after her unexpected still-birth.

3

Why Theology and Doctrine Matter in Children's Ministry

Right thinking for right living

JOHN PIPER

TRUTH, THEOLOGY, AND DOCTRINE. These are three terms that are so overlapping in my mind that I'm going to use them almost interchangeably. Here's the difference. Truth refers to the broadest statements that correspond with reality. That's what I mean by "truth." And then doctrine is the teaching of those statements, usually in some kind of organized way; a body of doctrine. Theology is when those statements are about God and His ways in the world. It's very simple; I don't have any sophisticated definitions, just statements that correspond with reality.

Everybody therefore does it, and you either do it well or you do it poorly, and our desire is that we do it well. I have two aims. The aim is, first, to persuade you from the Bible that there is such a thing as a body of doctrine there, to be transmitted to children as well as adults. And second, to argue that it matters enormously and to tell you why. So that's my two-point outline. But to go there, I want to give you, off my front burner, three illustrations of the kind of thing I mean.

Illustration Number One off my front burner is my devotions from this morning. I read the Bible through every year with the church, which is a good thing to encourage, along with Bible memory. This morning, in the New Testament, we were at 1 Corinthians 6:1-11, along with four other places in the Bible. I want to read you a portion of that, emphasizing a few words, and then ask you a few questions about your children's ministry by way of illustration.

> When one of you has a grievance against another, does he dare go to law before the unrighteous instead of the saints? Or do you not know that the saints will judge the world? And if the world is to be judged by you, are you incompetent to try trivial cases? Do you not know that we are to judge angels? How much more, then, matters pertaining to this life!

> To have lawsuits at all with one another is already a defeat for you. Why not rather suffer wrong? Why not rather be defrauded? But you yourselves wrong and defraud—even your own brothers!

> Or do you not know that the unrighteous will not inherit the kingdom of God? (1 Corinthians 6:1-3; 7-9a)

Do you not *know*? Do you not *know*? Do you not *know*? Right knowing produces right behavior. It must be you don't *know* something if you're suing each other. It must be you don't *know* something if your heart is so selfish, all you can imagine when you're wronged is to get back.

So I ask you, in regard to your children's ministry: Do the children of your church know, or do you have a plan for them to know, that they will judge the world? Do you have a plan for them to know that they will judge angels? Do you have a plan to explain to them what an angel is, and why some of them might need to be judged?

Or don't you care if they understand the Bible? Or make use of it not to sue each other when they become 18. Do you have a plan to help them know that the unrighteous will not enter the Kingdom of God?

Let's read verse 11. "Such were some of you. But you were washed. You were sanctified. You were justified in the name of the Lord Jesus and by the spirit of God." Do you have a plan so that they know what "I've been washed" means? How it is that you can say to a person, "Don't return evil for evil because those that return evil for evil won't go into the kingdom of heaven," and not undermine justification by faith alone?

Have you got the plan in place for building these little kids up into those who, when they're asked by the Apostle Paul, do you *know?*—They say, "Yes, and that's why we're not suing each other." "Yes, I know, and that's why I am not going to court before unbelievers." "Yes, I know, and that's why I am forgiving those who rip me off in my business. I was taught when I was four, you don't do that if you're a Christian, and you know God's going to hold them accountable, and God's forgiven me all my sins."

Knowing changes lives.

The Apostle Paul thinks it does. If you have not experienced that, or you go to a church where it's just doctrine and nobody is changed, and you draw the inference that doctrine doesn't change you, then throw your Bible away. Something else is going on there because the Bible says, "Do you not *know?* Do you not *know?* Do you not *know?*"

If you knew, you wouldn't sue each other. That's illustration number one off my front burner from devotions this morning.

Here's illustration number two. I was blown away, a few weeks ago, by reading *The Scandal of the Evangelical Conscience* by Ron Sider. The point of this 129-page book is this: *Evangelicals live like the world.* Statistic after statistic after statistic shows that we are not much different from the world. An evangelical is a person who says, "I have made a personal commitment to Jesus Christ that is still important in my life today, and I agree that Jesus lived a sinless life. Eternal salvation is only through grace, not works. Christians have a personal responsibility to evangelize non-Christians, and Satan exists." If you agree with that, you're an evangelical by this definition.[1]

Evangelicals divorce at about the same rate as the world. Nine percent of evangelicals tithe. Of 12,000 teenagers who took the pledge to wait for marriage, 80% of them had sex outside of marriage. Eighty

---

[1] Ronald J. Sider, *The Scandal of the Evangelical Conscience* (Grand Rapids: MI, Baker Books), 18.

percent of those evangelical kids who signed that they wouldn't, did. Twenty-six percent of traditional evangelicals don't think pre-marital sex is wrong. White evangelicals are more likely than Catholics and mainline Protestants to object to having a black neighbor.

Those numbers blew me away, and this began to settle me: Sider said, "George Barna has developed a set of criteria to identify people with a biblical worldview." In other words, they wanted to figure out, does it make any difference if you believe more of the Bible than just the minimum? These people believe, "the Bible is the moral standard" and also think that "absolute moral truths exist and are conveyed through the Bible." In addition, they agree with all six of the following additional beliefs:

- God is the all-knowing, all-powerful creator who still rules the universe.
- Jesus Christ lived a sinless life.
- Satan is a real living entity.
- Salvation is a free gift, not something we can earn.
- Every Christian has a personal responsibility to evangelize.
- The Bible is totally accurate in all it teaches.[2]

If you sign on to all those, they call you a person with a "biblical worldview." And then they discovered this:

The good news is that the small circle of people with a biblical world-view demonstrate genuinely different behavior. They are nine times more likely than all the others to avoid adult-only material on the internet. They are four times more likely than other Christians to boycott objectionable companies and products, and twice as likely to choose intentionally not to watch a movie, specifically because of its bad content.

They are three times more likely than other adults not to use tobacco products, and twice as likely to volunteer time to help needy people.

---

[2]   Ron Sider, 127.

Forty-nine percent of all born-again Christians with a biblical world-view have volunteered more than an hour in the previous week to an organization serving the poor. Whereas 29% of born-again Christians without a biblical worldview, and only 22% of non born-again Christians have done so.[3]

Here's his important conclusion:

Barna's findings on the different behavior of Christians with a biblical worldview underline the importance of theology. Biblical orthodoxy does matter. One important way to end the scandal of the contemporary Christian behavior is to work and pray fervently for the growth of orthodox theological belief in our churches.[4]

In other words, to grow up kids who will be different from the world is *to work*. It's hard work. *And pray* fervently for the growth of orthodox theological belief in our churches. It takes God.

Illustration number three: I gave a talk on Saint Athanasius a few weeks ago, and as I was thinking about him and John Owen and J. Gresham Machen, and Spurgeon, and people in our own day, I was finding that Satan's tactics are not very different from age to age.

Athanasius was the fourth-century defender of the deity of Christ, the author of the First Council of Nicaea. When you say the Nicene Creed, most of those words come from Athanasius. And I draw from him, over and against so much of contemporary, postmodern thinking in the church, this statement, "Loving Christ includes loving true propositions about Christ."

"Loving Christ includes—cannot be separated from—*loving* true propositions." If you make fun of true propositions about Jesus, you blaspheme. If you belittle propositions that accurately describe the King of Kings, you are treacherous. To assert things like, "There was a time when the Son of God was not," is blasphemy.

Arius was saying, "He was not, before he was made." This is what Athanasius fought against with all this might. Or, here's another

---

[3] Sider, 128.
[4] Sider, 129.

proposition: "The Son of God is created." Now, those propositions are strictly damnable. If we encourage people to embrace them, or don't *dis*courage people from embracing them, we damn them.

We hand them over to propositions that, if they embrace them, will send them to hell. I think Athanasius would have abominated with tears the contemporary call that may even be in some of your churches, for "de-propositionalizing," or, "reforming," or becoming "post-evangelical"—these are all catch phrases for the people who are moving away from what I'm arguing for.

I think Athanasius would have said to them, "Our young people in Alexandria die for the truth, the propositions about Christ. What do your young people die for?"

And if the answer comes back, which I suspect it would—"We die for Christ, not propositions about Christ"—I think Athanasius would have said, "That's exactly the way the heretic Arius talks. Which Christ," Athanasius would ask, "do they die for?"

To answer the question, "which Christ are you going to die for?" you must make a proposition about Jesus. You must say something about Him. And to refuse to answer that question, which is the most common contemporary tactic, is to say, "It doesn't matter what Christ you die for—that word can stand for anything you want it to." This is damnable.

I'm worked up about this issue—about standing firm on truth —because doctrine and theology really matter.

First, there is a body of doctrine, truth, theology to be passed on to children. And there are three texts to defend the truth that there is a body of doctrine. Romans 6:17 says, "Thanks be to God that you who were once slaves of sin have become obedient, from the heart, to the standard of teaching by which you were committed." "Standard of teaching" implies there's a body, there's a group of teachings. He says, "I'm so thankful to God that you, Romans, from the heart—it's not just head knowledge—have been committed to the standard of teaching. Already in the New Testament, before we can have the whole New Testament to build on, there was emerging this body of teaching that Paul wanted to make sure all believers came to know.

The second text is Acts 20:27: "I did not shrink from declaring to you the whole counsel of God." This is Paul saying that his conscience is clear. He is leaving the Ephesian elders. He will probably never see them again, and he says, "my conscience is clear because I didn't shrink from declaring to you *the whole counsel of God*." That phrase, along with "standard of teaching," implies there's a body of doctrine, a body of truth called *the whole counsel of God.*

Paul is saying, "I didn't leave anything essential out. I taught you, and now my hands are free from your blood." Are you willing to say that about the children who spend as many as 12 years in your ministry? When you're done, will you be able to say, "Your blood is not on my hands; I have taught you the whole counsel of God"—as much as they can take in that age?

The third text is 2 Timothy 1:13-14. "Follow the pattern of the sound words that you have heard from me, in the faith and love that are in Christ Jesus. By the Holy Spirit who dwells within us, guard the good deposit entrusted to you." Here Paul uses two phrases for it: "the pattern of sound words" and "the good deposit entrusted to you."

Let me give you all four phrases: "standard of teaching," "whole counsel of God," "pattern of sound words," "good deposit entrusted to you." And I hope you agree with me that there is something being pointed to there that we should care deeply about handing on to every new believer, no matter what age, and especially to our own descendants as they grow up in our homes and in our church.

Now let me give you an illustration of Paul's attitude toward this body of doctrine. We've seen three places where he says there is such a thing. Let's look at two passages of Scripture, one from Galatians 1 and one from Philippians 1, and ask: why the difference in tone? Here's Galatians 1:6-8,

I'm astonished—[In fact, astonished is an understatement. This is the one letter that has no loving salutation at the front end. He just jumps in; he's really upset with what's going on in the churches of Galatia.] I'm astonished that you are so quickly deserting Him who called you in the grace of Christ and are turning to a different gospel. Not that there is another one, but there are some who trouble you and want to distort the gospel of Christ, but even—[Now get this, this is as strong as he can say it,]—even if we or an angel from heaven should preach to you another gospel contrary to what we preached to you, let him be cursed.

Damn him!—Now that's strong language, and what perplexes me about the Apostle Paul is why he didn't use that same language in Philippians 1.

In Philippians 1:15-18, Paul's in prison, and there are these rascals, these seemingly loveless rascals, trying to make his imprisonment more burdensome by preaching what he can't preach. He loves to preach, and he can't preach, and so they're going to preach instead and make him feel awful.

So listen to how Paul says it:

Some indeed preach Christ from envy—[Now, that's a bad way to preach Christ!]—Some indeed preach Christ from envy and rivalry, but others from good will. The latter do it out of love, knowing that I'm put here for the defense of the gospel. The former proclaim Christ out of rivalry, not sincerely.—[Whew! They're not sincere preachers of the Gospel.]—not sincerely, but thinking to afflict me in my imprisonment. What then?—[Well, damn them. Damn them!]—What then? Only that in every way, whether in pretense or truth, Christ is proclaimed and in that I rejoice.

What's going on here? Calling down divine curses in Galatia and rejoicing in jail in regard to the Philippians? Here's the difference: There's not a whiff of implication in Philippians that they were getting the message wrong.

That's the whole point of Galatians 1: Another gospel was being preached. But let this land on you because this is *so different* from today and the evangelical church. Today, what gets people *really* worked up? Bad attitudes. Bad relationships. You start preaching out of envy? You be damned! We are keen on condemning bad attitudes, and then we just whitewash whether the message is right or not. No big deal. It's the attitude that counts.

I'm not defending envy. I'm not defending rivalry. I'm just saying it is incredible to me that Paul, sitting in jail, knowing that their attitude stinks, would rejoice that they're preaching! Isn't that incredible? Would I do that? I am so 20th century, pragmatic-American, relational-saturated. I would preach against that attitude and say, "That's not the essence of the Gospel! A bad attitude is a contradiction of the Gospel!" So, what's wrong with Paul?

Nothing. Nothing is wrong with him. He's just got things in order: Truth first. Attitude second. And if truth is happening out there, and their attitude is bad—I'm going to praise God that truth is happening. But if they switch their message, I'm calling down a curse on them.

That's big. I think that's really big. There is a body of truth and we ought to make sure we know it, love it, share it.

Here's point number two: In the New Testament, it really matters that we transmit this truth, this doctrine, this theology, this body, this teaching, to the next generation. It really matters, and I've got five reasons and I'll put them in the form of questions.

DO YOU WANT THE CHILDREN IN YOUR MINISTRY TO COME TO A DEEP, STRONG, UNSHAKEABLE FAITH AND BE SAVED FROM SIN AND HELL?

Do you what them to come to unshakeable, lighthouse-like-on-rock faith and thus be saved from sin, guilt, death, hell? And, of course, your answer is "yes."

My simple observation is that the Word of God rightly taught does that.

First consider Romans 10:17. "So faith comes from hearing, and hearing through the word of Christ." Little ears! Little ears! Where does faith come from for those little ears? It comes from hearing, and hearing by the word of Christ. And I'm going to say, the word of Christ *rightly understood*. Not "Christ is a doorknob." Or, "Christ is not divine." Or, "Christ is a Hindu guru." When it says "by the word of Christ" it means the biblical Christ—the doctrinally sound Christ.

Text number two, 1 Timothy 4:16. "Keep a close watch on yourself and on the teaching. Persist in this, for by so doing you will save both yourself and your hearers." Do you want to ensure the salvation of these little children who hear you? If you do, pay attention to your teaching and persevere in it because by your teaching, your soul is saved and their soul is saved. I couldn't say it much more clearly. Right teaching saves souls.

Third text, Acts 20:26-27. Speaking to the Ephesian elders, Paul says, "Therefore I testify to you this day that I am innocent of the blood of all, for I did not shrink from declaring to you the whole counsel of God." Do you want to be able to say this when your work is done in the ministry to children in your church? You've given the years to it; you've done your best. Do you want to be able to say, "I am innocent of the blood of all"? Which, by the way, means you can't guarantee their salvation by right teaching. Some of these kids are going to be lost, and you will have done your job right.

Last text on this point, 2 Thessalonians 2:9-10. "The coming of the lawless one is by the activity of Satan with all power and false signs and wonders, and with all wicked deception for those who are perishing, because they refused to love the truth and so be saved." The lawless one is the antichrist at the end of the age. What saves? The love of the truth. The ones who are perishing wouldn't receive it. A loving presentation and exalting in the truth was presented to them in Sunday school and high school ministry and in the pew, and they wouldn't have it. They wouldn't receive the truth and love the truth. And they perish. Paul connects perishing with refusing a love for the truth. Which makes me tremble for those evangelicals today who play fast and loose with propositions.

That's question number one. Under the evidence, it really matters. It matters because the Word—the teaching—awakens faith.

I can hear two objections because I bump into them all the time. Objection number one: Doesn't this emphasis on the truth minimize the work of the Holy Spirit? It doesn't minimize the work of the Holy Spirit. It agrees with the Holy Spirit in putting Him in His favorite place. What's the favorite place of the Holy Spirit? It's right behind the preaching of the Gospel as it moves, like a jet, through the world. You've seen those four jets, the Thunderbirds, and they're just amazing. Vroom. Vroom. Like they've got a rod attached between them. They keep in such perfect formation. Well, the one in the front is the preaching of the Gospel, and the one in the back is the Holy Spirit.

Vroom. Vroom. Vroom. If the one in front says, "I don't think I want to go to Afghanistan," guess what? The Holy Spirit won't go either.

The Holy Spirit is in the world to glorify Jesus. In John 16:14, Jesus says, "He will glorify me. For he will take what is mine and declare it to you." This means the Holy Spirit likes to be tucked right in behind Christ-exalting teaching, Christ-exalting devotions, Christ-exalting prayers, Christ-exalting preaching, Christ-exalting lives. Wherever Christ is exalted with the mouth, the Holy Spirit moves. But if you shut your mouth, and go back home, and pray, He will not move. He will not do an end-run around the Word of Truth, around the Gospel.

The second objection is, "Aren't you minimizing the role of prayer?" I was asked to speak years ago at a missions conference, and they assigned me the title "Prayer: The Work of Missions." So I stood up, and my first sentence was, "Prayer: The Work of Missions—it's not." Nobody gets saved by prayer alone. Preaching the Gospel is the work of missions, and prayer is the handmaid of the Gospel. The Gospel must be preached, and the Gospel is the exultation of Christ, and when the Holy Spirit sees Christ being exulted and lifted up, He moves on people to say, "Look at him!" and He opens their heart. Nobody gets saved without the sovereign Spirit of God changing their hearts.

I've prayed for unbelievers all my life, and I still do, just like Paul says in Romans 10:1, "My heart's desire and prayer to God for them is that they might be saved." I have people in my life that I love so deeply I would die for their salvation. But, when I read the New Testament and look for how the Bible teaches prayer in relation to evangelism, it's almost uniform in the New Testament that we pray for the speaker, not the hearer:

"...pray earnestly to the Lord of the Harvest to send laborers..." (Matthew 9:38)

Finally, brothers, pray for us, that the word of the Lord may speed ahead and be honored...(2 Thessalonians 3:1)

Pray also for us, that God may open to us a door for the word...(Colossians 4:3)

[Pray] also for me, that the words may be given to me in opening my mouth boldly to proclaim the mystery of the gospel...as I ought to speak (Ephesians 6:19, 20b).

It's almost uniform in the New Testament that we pray for the speaker, not the hearer. Almost. Romans 10:1 is an exception, and I'm glad it's an exception. I want to pray for lost people, and I should. But mainly the New Testament illustrates prayer is for preachers and teachers and sharers of the Gospel—that the Holy Spirit would come upon them, just like it did in Acts 4:31. It says, "they were all filled with the Holy Spirit and they spoke the Word of God with boldness." That's what happens when the Holy Spirit comes upon a church. People start speaking unashamedly in the church and outside the church, and then the Holy Spirit really moves in power because he loves to magnify Jesus being lifted up in the Gospel.

So, my response to those objections is "No, no, no, no!" In teaching that the Word saves—that right understanding of the Gospel saves—I'm not minimizing the Holy Spirit. He has his favorite place empowering the Word right behind the word. And I'm not minimizing prayer because God has ordained that the Holy Spirit move upon the preacher for the sake of the heart by prayer.

DO YOU WANT YOUR CHILDREN TO BE SANCTIFIED AND FREED FROM THE BONDAGE OF SIN?

John 17:17 says, "Sanctify them in the truth. Your word is truth." That is a prayer. Now you have the two coming together. Lord, take these kids and sanctify them; in every biblical sense of setting them apart for yourself and of morally transforming their lives in accordance with Jesus. Sanctify these kids in the truth. How in the world will God answer that prayer if you shut your mouth and give them a truncated Gospel, little fragments, little pieces?

John 8:32, says, "You will know the truth and the truth will make you free."

2 Peter 1:3-4, says:

His divine power has granted to us all things that pertain to life and godliness, through the knowledge of him who called us to his own glory and excellence, by which he has granted to us his precious and very great promises, so that through them you may become partakers of the divine nature, having escaped from the corruption that is in the world because of sinful desire.

That's an amazing passage of Scripture in how to escape from corruption, how to be shaped into the character of God, and how to have power for godliness—namely, knowledge of Him, knowledge of His glory, knowledge of His excellence, knowledge of His promises, and banking on them. I wrote a whole book on that called *Future Grace* which is my way of saying, "Standing on the promises you cannot fail" to become holier than you were if you didn't.

When you teach children biblical doctrine, what do you do? You put in their hands the one offensive weapon of the biblical armor in Ephesians 6, namely the sword, which is the Word of God. Then you go over to Romans 8:12-13, "We are debtors not to the flesh, to live according to the flesh. For if you live according to the flesh, you will die, but if, by the Spirit, you put to death the deeds of the body, you will live." Well, what's in my hand for putting to death the deeds of the body? I'll tell you what it is, it's the sword of the Spirit. That's what's in my hand. If we take this out of our kid's hands, they are sitting ducks for the devil. But if we put arrows in their quiver and swords and daggers in their scabbards, they'll have one tailor-made for every demonic temptation, and they can duke the devil.

DO YOU WANT YOUR CHILDREN, THE CHILDREN IN YOUR MINISTRY, TO BE FREED FROM THE POWER OF SATAN?

There's a text that has proved to be massively significant in how I think about demonic oppression. I've been corresponding with a man who has a 9-year-old, and he believes his son is demon oppressed. And oh, how I've been counseling and praying. I just got an email the day before yesterday in which he said, "I think he's past it. He's been normal for a couple of months." It was an awful, dark season.

2 Timothy 2:24-26, says,

And the Lord's servant must not be quarrelsome but kind to everyone, able to teach, patiently enduring evil, correcting his opponents with gentleness. God may perhaps grant them repentance leading to a knowledge of the truth, and they may come to their senses and escape from the snare of the devil, after being captured by him to do his will.

This text addresses us because it says, okay, children's worker, you've got some kids that seem to be picking up on that black, dark stuff at home that causes people to kill 10 people in Redwing, Minnesota. That dark demonic stuff—this kid just seems to have it. What are you going to do? What's your strategy?

Well, I want this to be in your quiver: "The Lord's servant must not be quarrelsome but kind...able to teach, patiently enduring evil." This kid is not going to treat you nice. You will need to be correcting with gentleness. God may grant him repentance and an escape from the snare of the devil through your loving teaching, your patient correction. It doesn't *sound* supernatural; it *is* supernatural.

If you trust God, and say, "Oh God, when I walk in there this morning, let there be an anointing on me so that as I open my mouth and talk about Jesus Christ, crucified and risen and triumphant, as I go to that little passage of Scripture where He said to the devil, "Go" and people said, "Look, he commands the unclean spirits and they come out of him. What kind of authority is this?" I pray that that little child would be delivered through my words. It is supernatural though the Word.

DO YOU WANT THE CHILDREN IN YOUR MINISTRY TO ABOUND IN LOVE, AND NOT JUST AVOID BAD BEHAVIOR?

It's so sad that we give kids in churches lists of dos and don'ts. When they come to us and say, "What's wrong with this music?" What do we teach them? How do we challenge them? When my boys said that, and they all did, I'd say, "It's the wrong question. I'm not interested in giving you a longer list. The right question is, 'Is it helping you pray? Is it helping you love Jesus? Is it helping you be kind to people, and love people, and bless people, and hate sin and be humble, and hate pride, and get free from your lock-step conformity to the teenage world? Is it helping you?' That's the question I want you to ask, Son." Philippians 1:9 says, "This I pray, that your love may abound still more and more in real knowledge and all discernment." "I'm praying for you, Son, that your love for people, for the Lord, will abound more and more in or by knowledge, and all discernment."

DO WE WANT OUR CHILDREN TO BE HAPPY IN GOD NOW AND FOREVER?

In John 15:11, Jesus says, "These things I have spoken to you that my joy may be in you, and that your joy may be full."

Jesus is God. He could have just reached out and touched Peter on the chest, and he would have been the happiest person in the universe. But He chose to do it another way. Words. Isn't that amazing? I never cease to be amazed that we have become Christians, and that we become holy, and that we get free from sin. We get free from the devil! We become loving, and now we become happy by the Word! It is so sad when you see churches where the Bible is almost gone—where they preach another message, do children's ministries another way—when the most staggering things happen when that Word goes into people's heads and hearts.

"These things I have spoken to you." Do you wake up sad in the morning? Jesus said, "I've said some things that would make you happy. Go, read them, and ask me to do what I said I would do." That's the way I fight the fight of faith. I'm not by nature a happy person. I wouldn't write all these books about seeking happiness if I were happy! I'm a very melancholy and struggling person, and I love Jesus saying, "Piper, for you and your kids and this church; I've said some things to you, that my joy may be in you, and your joy may be full."

I wrote a little book called *God is the Gospel*. And what's behind that title is me looking back over these five reasons for the importance of the Word and doctrine and theology and truth, and saying, "Why should I care about being saved? Why should I care about being a loving person? Why should I care about having faith? Why should I care about escaping sin, Satan, hell?" *Well, hell hurts. That's why.* Bad answer. Really bad answer. It's not a God-glorifying answer, it's a flesh glorifying answer. "I don't want to go to hell; it hurts!" Oh, so your skin is really valuable, right? Yeah. So what else? Anything else valuable? "Well, I just don't want to hurt." That's not a good answer, right? I'm driven by Gospel sentence after Gospel sentence to ask, "Why is this good news, ultimately?" And my answer is, it gets me to God. And if God isn't my treasure, there is no Gospel in the Bible. If God Himself is not why I want out of Hell and into Heaven, I'm not going there.

And therefore, I want to lead my kids, not only in all these things, I want to lead them to have God. Not just have joy in the abstract. Or to have justification. Or to have forgiveness of sins. Or to have sanctification. Or to have love. I don't want them to just have those things. I want them to have God.

Along with all this elevation of truth and elevation of doctrine and elevation of theology, which I consider indispensable, I'm going to love these kids, and I'm going to spend time with these kids, and I'm going to play with these kids on the living room rug, or on the Sunday school floor. And I'm going to hug these kids, and I'm going to care for their every physical and emotional need, and I'm going to surround them with all kinds of godly influences, and I'm going to take them to church, and I'm going to celebrate with joy every sliver of grace—common grace and special grace—in their lives. And I'm going to provide for them strong God-like security, and firmness, and sweetness, and I'm going to pray for them. I'm going to do all that. And then, I'm going to read this verse.

> Whoever abides in the teaching, has both the Father and the Son
> (2 John 9b).

Whoever abides in the teaching *has* God. And if you don't, you don't. And that would be the greatest sadness of all. But if you do, you do. And that would be the greatest gladness of all. All you precious children's workers, stand on the truth, firm. Realize, and manifest in your ministries, that it really matters: doctrine, theology, truth. Word.

JOHN PIPER pastored Bethlehem church in Minneapolis, MN for almost 33 years and founded Desiring God ministries. He is married to Noël, and they have five grown children and 12 grandchildren.

4

The Fullness of
the Whole
Counsel of God

From grand story to grammar, it all matters

BRUCE A. WARE

"Therefore I testify to you this day that I am innocent of the blood of all, for I did not shrink from declaring to you the whole counsel of God" (Acts 20:26-27).

WHEN PAUL WRITES, "I did not shrink from declaring the whole counsel of God," the word *shrink* indicates his resolution; his determined commitment to declare all the aspects of God's Word, even those that are difficult to share with others.

Along with what is smooth and soft and comfortable in our teaching and preaching at times also comes sharp edges intended to bless those to whom this difficult message is given. The uncomfortable, unpopular, unwanted, unwelcome, the potentially offensive—must be proclaimed, must be declared along with what is desired, expected, and welcome.

The Apostle Paul, as he did this, did so with winsomeness, with charity—even in those occasions where he had to speak sternly. He did it in a way that tried to commend to his hearers the goodness and wisdom of following the ways of God and was never over-the-top in hurting people. He did not write *to* offend even when what he wrote *did* offend. He wrote to build up through the difficult words he sometimes had to speak.

What does this mean for us, that we, too, are to declare the fullness of the whole counsel of God to others? I suggest we consider two categories, namely, the breadth and depth of the whole counsel of God.

THE BREADTH OF GOD'S WORD— BOOK BY BOOK

First, we need to be a people who comes to understand the whole of biblical content, book by book, through the whole of the Bible. One of the goals each of us should have is to think through the basic flow of the content of each of the 66 books of the Bible. Beginning in Genesis, for example, think through, where does it start, how does it progress, what are the key figures, who are the main people, what main events take place? Can I track through the progression of the book of Genesis? What happens in Exodus? Can I follow the development of the book of Exodus? On we go through the Bible. This is within our grasp, and it would be helpful if each of us could think through every book of the Bible.

One tool that helps is a good study Bible. An advantage of a good study Bible is that you can get an introduction to the book, understand some of the historical background, and learn who the audience is. This will help you better understand the flow of what happens in various books of the Bible. May God help us to have as one of the goals in our lives to grow in an understanding of the content of every book of the Bible.

THE BREADTH OF GOD'S WORD— THE GRAND STORY

Second, we grow in breadth of God's Word as we understand the whole of the Bible story line—not just the development that takes place in each book separately, but what unfolds in the Bible as a whole, as one coherent book, one unified story.

Isn't it amazing that behind every author of the Bible there is One Author who superintended everything that takes place? As Peter reminds us, no prophecy of Scripture is a matter of the human author's own origination, but men moved by the Holy Spirit spoke from God (see 2 Peter 1:20-21). This One author, this Divine Author, assures us that there is a unity to the whole of the Bible. There is a continuity, an intentional development of truth that comes through the whole of the Bible. We don't have 66 books that are in conflict with each other where we have to decide which ones we're going to accept. We have a uniform Bible.

Here are anchor points that constitute key elements in the development of the storyline of the Bible. Think of them as if you're going across a very long bridge. There have to be, at points along the way, supports that go down deep into the ground, that hold the bridge up all the way across.

CREATION —God made everything. How important that is in understanding both God and us.

FALL —God created a good world, but it was messed up terribly because of the sin that happened in Genesis 3.

COVENANT —Although we're fallen, God chooses to come to us; to establish covenant with sinners who deserve only His judgment. It begins with Noah, we see it with Abraham, and it's a key concept as you move through the Bible.

ELECTION —Do you think of "election" when you think of Abraham? You ought to. Who chose whom? God picked Abraham; then Isaac, not Ishmael; then Jacob, not Esau.

ISRAEL —God chooses a small tribe of people to be His own. How important the people of Israel are in the unfolding of the storyline of the Bible.

THE OTHER NATIONS THAT SURROUND ISRAEL—Egypt, Babylon, Assyria, Edom, Amon, Moab. These countries play a pivotal role in the unfolding storyline of the Bible.

BONDAGE—The people of Israel, God's people of promise, are enslaved in Egypt.

DELIVERANCE—This theme is given beautiful display in the Exodus of the people of Israel out of Egypt; it continues as a dominant theme through the rest of the Bible.

LAW—What other people on the face of the earth were given the privilege of having the very Word of God given to them? Do you think of the law this way? I hope you do. If the people live this Word, they will experience fullness of life. But if they depart from this Word, they will bring upon themselves untold misery.

PROMISE—Though God's people broke the law, He promises them a day in which He will once again show His mercy and kindness to those who have brought upon themselves only His just judgment. Notice in the prophets, the final word that God has for His people is not His word of judgment. He gives that elsewhere, over and over! But His final word is a word of restoration, of renewal, of salvation; the promise and hope of His goodness and kindness to them.

KINGDOM—The kingdom of Israel becomes the platform for the coming Messiah.

JUDGMENT—Understanding God's righteous action against rebellious sinners is key to understanding the flow of biblical history, including the story of God's merciful salvation.

CROSS—Here we are at the pinnacle of the outworking of God's redemptive purposes.

T Y P E—Do you know this word? A lot of Christians have not learned it. In the Bible we not only have prophecy and fulfillment, but we also have typology—either a person, or an object, or an event which happens at one point in the Old Testament that anticipates a repetition of that same person, object, or event in greater measure later, sometimes several times, before you get to the fullest expression of it. So, King David is not only the first of the kings that gives rise to Jesus, the ultimate King—in that sense it's prophecy and fulfillment—but it's typology that the Christ who comes is the greater David. David will sit upon the throne of his people, says the prophet Ezekiel. Well, David has been dead a long time. How can David sit upon his throne? It's the greater David. This is type and fulfillment.

C H U R C H—Not the same as Israel. There is continuity, yes; similarities, yes, but this is a new thing. "I will build my church," declares Jesus in Matthew 16:18. Jew and Gentile brought together in one body in Christ.

W I T N E S S—Before His ascension, Jesus told his disciples to wait in Jerusalem for the what the Father promised. "...you will receive power when the Holy Spirit has come upon you, and you will be my witnesses in Jerusalem and in all Judea and Samaria, and to the ends of the earth" (Acts 1:8).

W O R S H I P—What are we here for as the people of God? What will we do forever, with incredible joy and energy? We are worshippers of the one true and living God, who worship in the Spirit of God and glory in Christ Jesus (Philippians 3:3).

H O L I N E S S—Notice the repeated pattern in Israel: called to be holy, yet failing to be holy. So the Holy Spirit is given to work within the hearts of sinful people to make us what we are not, to produce the holiness we cannot produce.

FAITHFULNESS—It is required of a steward that he be found faithful (1 Corinthians 4:2). Standing before Christ on the day of judgment, the question will be, "Have you been faithful with what God has given you?"

ALIEN—What does it mean to be a holy people? Separated, so we're not like the rest of those out there. But we want to be like everyone else, don't we? That's our sin. God calls us to be holy, to be aliens.

SUFFERING—This is part of life as the people of God.

CONSUMMATION—The fulfillment of all that will surely, certainly occur when Christ comes again and establishes the new creation in fullness.

SEPARATION—When Jesus returns in glory, He will separate all the peoples like a shepherd separates sheep and goats (Matthew 25:31-46). The goats will be separated from God, away from the presence of the Lord and the glory of His power (2 Thessalonians 1:9). God alone has goodness, joy, truth—everything that fills and satisfies the human heart. Being away from His presence and the glory of His power is the most horrible thing that could happen.

HELL—Everlasting condemnation, torment, and judgment that comes to pass for all unbelievers in the end.

HEAVEN—Joy, everlasting life, never-ending satisfaction that is ours, in the presence of God, forever and ever.

Every one of these are anchor points. And there are more: The Greater Moses, Messiah, King, Prophet, Priest, Sacrifice, Triumph, Pentecost, the list goes on. They have one place in the Bible where they begin, but then they repeat over and over again. They become part of the very fabric—the furniture of the house that we call the Bible. Can you think through the storyline of the Bible and these anchor point themes along the way? May God help us see the overarching storyline of the Bible, the flow of the Bible from beginning to end, so that we can develop a Christian worldview.

THE DEPTH OF GOD'S WORD— PASSAGES OF SCRIPTURE

First, we need to grow in an in-depth understanding of passages of Scripture so that we become not only better at understanding the flow of thought in books of the Bible, but also able to go deep in passages. We need to learn to study the Bible; to read the Bible attentively with clear observation of what is there.

I commend to you two ways of growing in your reading of God's Word. First, as we are encouraged to do at the beginning of a new year, we must read through the whole Bible consistently so we familiarize ourselves regularly with both Testaments and what is contained throughout all of the Bible. A good Bible reading plan that we follow over a year or two instructs us and reminds us of the "big picture" of the Bible. There is simply no substitute for this "fast" reading of the whole of the Bible, year by year, decade by decade.

While this fast reading of the Bible is necessary, it is also important and deeply soul-enriching to learn to read the Bible slowly. That is, we must also read shorter portions of Scripture over and over, meditating thoughtfully and prayerfully on the details that are there, in order to see and be moved by the glory and beauty of God's Word. You probably know the phrase "the devil is in the details." Here's another phrase for you: "the *glory* is in the details." Look at the "for," the "because," the "and;" the connectors of sections of Scripture; the parts of speech; the plain meaning of words and the grammar. The small details make a big difference in meaning.

It would take many lifetimes to be able to meditate on every bit of the Bible. So you have to be selective in the passages you choose for meditation. Take particular parts that are rich and of special importance for doing that pondering work, that meditative work, where you think through and understand with greater detail what is taught there.

Second, we need not only an in-depth understanding of passages of Scripture, but an in-depth understanding of the doctrines of Scripture.

THE DEPTH OF GOD'S WORD—
DOCTRINES OF SCRIPTURE

I've spent most of my life probing doctrines of the Bible, and here's what I have found: In every major doctrine of the Christian faith, there are truths within each that are tremendously offensive to our culture. I think this is why you see so much compromise taking place by so-called professing evangelicals who come up with new ways of understanding these doctrines. What they are doing is adapting the doctrine to fit the culture.

The elite of the educated people in society have long looked at the Bible and Christian theology and thought it to be a bit ridiculous. In 1799, Friedrich Schleiermacher, the father of modern liberalism, wrote *On Religion: Speeches to its Cultured Despisers*, where he revamped theology in a way that made it fit with the intuitions, values, and commitments of the elite within the culture. He proposed that we reshape the Bible and the Christian faith to fit the culture. My friends, we cannot stand before God on the day of judgment and hold our heads high if we do that.

There are areas in every doctrine of the faith that are offensive to the culture, so we need a resolute commitment: We will go with the Bible and its teaching. If it doesn't agree with the culture, we ought not be surprised. God told us from the beginning it would be this way. "For the word of the cross is folly to those who are perishing, but to us who are being saved it is the power of God" (1 Corinthians 1:18).

Let me walk through some areas of doctrine with you to remind you how important it is to know these glorious truths.

Let's start with the doctrine of God. I can't imagine anything more significant than getting God right. Here's how A. W. Tozer put it in *The Knowledge of the Holy*, "What comes into our minds when we think about God is the most important thing about us."[1] What a great opening sentence! Tozer is absolutely right. Everything else flows from your understanding of God.

---

[1]   A. W. Tozer, *The Knowledge of the Holy* (New York, NY: Harper Collins, 1961), 1.

TRANSCENDENCE AND IMMANENCE OF GOD—Remarkably, God is immanently connected to his people. That is, God is close at hand, nearby; He is the God who comes to us with comfort, mercy, grace, kindness, love, generosity, and forgiveness. But, while God is the God of immanent care, He is also the God of transcendent holiness, otherness, separateness. We have produced, largely speaking, a Christian culture in North America that rushes to immanence. When we talk about attributes of God in our preaching and singing, we over-emphasize the love of God, the kindness of God, the mercy and the grace of God. This isn't wrong, but it isn't complete and accurate if we don't understand *first* that God is transcendently glorious, separate from us, in no need of any of us. He did not create the world because He was lonely and needed a friend to fill up the void in His life. No, the Trinitarian God—Father, Son, and Holy Spirit—is infinitely and eternally filled with joy. The fellowship within the trinity far surpasses anything God could have with finite creatures. He is the excellent, perfect, glorious, transcendent, eternal, self-existent, self-sufficient God—who then loves the likes of us!

Transcendence and then immanence, in that order. Consider Isaiah 6. Isaiah saw the Lord, seated on his throne, lofty, exalted, with the train of robe filling the temple. The Seraphim cried out, "Holy, Holy, Holy!" And it was only after Isaiah saw God's transcendent majesty that he could also see his own misery—"Woe is me! For I am lost; for I am a man of unclean lips, and I dwell in the midst of a people of unclean lips; for my eyes have seen the King, the LORD of hosts!" (Isaiah 6:5). What comes next is astonishing. This glorious, transcendent God then showed Isaiah his immanent care and mercy. He brought him forgiveness and called him into His service. Such is the immanence of a God who is infinitely glorious—who doesn't need to do what He did in showing this forgiveness to Isaiah.

Transcendence first. Then immanence. We need to see they're both true, but there's an order in the Bible.

ATTRIBUTES OF GOD—Another category under the doctrine of God we must grow in understanding is the whole range of the attributes of God. Do you know the terms incommunicable and communicable attributes? Incommunicable are those divine attributes that are God's alone; they are not shared with us. Communicable attributes are true of God, but God has chosen to share these, in finite measure, with us as well. For example: "Be holy as I am holy," love as God loves, show compassion as God shows compassion, exercise justice in ways that God exercises justice. Marvel both at attributes true of God alone, and those He graciously grants us to share in as well.

PROVIDENCE OF GOD —We need also to understand divine providence in the doctrine of God. This is so important for everyday life, but it really shows up when suffering takes place. When there are difficulties and trials in your life, or the life of a friend, or a family member, how do you understand God's relation to that difficulty that you're facing? Is He distant from it, saying, "Oh, I'm so sorry that's happening! But I'll comfort you in it." Or, is He the one who ordains the very suffering we experience for the purpose of growing us up and seeing good purposes accomplished, which never would happen apart from that suffering?

Hebrews 5:8-9, says, "Although he was a son"—this is Jesus—"he learned obedience through what he suffered. And being made perfect, he became the source of eternal salvation to all who obey him." Here's the bottom line of those two verses. If Jesus had not undergone the growth process through suffering that was directed to Him by the Father's design, He would not have been able to go to the cross. He went to the cross only through the pathway of growing through suffering. My friends, instead of thinking, "God is not in this affliction; He feels as badly about this as I do," doesn't it make all the difference to know, "God is in this; He ordained this for good purposes"? What hope there is in that understanding of the greatness of God who ordains even affliction for the sake of the good He will bring about in His people.

HUMANITY AND SIN —We need to understand the doctrines of humanity and sin. I separate these two because though every one of us are human sinners, to be human is not to be a sinner. We are the defiled version of humanity. We're the junkyard version, not the showroom (new from the factory, without defect) version. Adam was the showroom version. Even better is the Second Adam, who perfectly displays true humanity.

Humanity as it ought to be, as God created it to be—the goodness, the glory, the wisdom, the beauty of humanity created in the image of God—that's Jesus; that's the original Adam. In our sin, we have a spoiled, marred version of that. By God's grace, what He's doing is reclaiming for us true humanity, unaffected by sin. He's getting rid of the disease. He's removing the cancer. Cancer is not an integral part of who we are, it's an intruder, an alien presence that ought to be ripped out of us. Sin is like cancer. It's not an integral part of humanity, though it is a pervasive part of all of our humanity. But in His mercy, God is working to rid us of that sin.

There are two sides to this; first, the goodness of humanity. God created us good. Genesis 1:31 says, "God looked at everything He had made and behold, it was very good." To see that is to realize that God had good designs in human sexuality, in the human body, in human relationships—these were all designed good. We should not dismiss human sexuality or the body or human relationships as intrinsically immoral or inescapably evil. No! We need to reclaim the goodness of what God designed in the beginning. Sin has corrupted it, but in Christ, we can grow, experiencing more of the good that God designed in us from the very beginning.

Second, the incredible corrupting power of sin. Sin takes hold of an unbeliever so powerfully that the Bible describes an unbeliever as a *slave* to sin, under Satan's power. In 2 Timothy 2, Paul tells Timothy to be gentle with those that oppose him, that "God may perhaps grant them repentance leading to a knowledge of the truth, and they may come to their senses and escape from the snare of the devil, after being captured by him to do his will" (25-26).

Every unbeliever you see is enslaved to Satan. They are capable of doing only one thing before God, and that is sin. They can sin in a variety of ways, but that is all they can do. Do you know why it's so important to see this, the pervasiveness of the power of sin that holds us in slavery, and the guilt and condemnation that sin brings upon us? Because we will only understand the glory of grace, of salvation, of freedom from the bondage of sin, and forgiveness from the guilt of sin, when we understand how bad sin is.

Think of how many churches never talk about sin because they don't want to discourage their people. It is mind-boggling how they could miss this. It's like a medical doctor whose specialty is treating various forms of cancer. A patient comes in and the doctor thinks, *I don't want to discourage that person and talk about cancer with him. I'm just going to tell him good things. I want him to leave my office feeling good about himself.* Malpractice, right?! We would all agree with that.

It's the same thing for those who pretend to preach the Word of God but do not help people, grown-ups and children alike, see how bad their problem is. Without a true understanding of their problem, they will have no context for seeing how glorious the solution is in Christ.

CHRIST—In Christology, one of the things I have seen that is really helpful in understanding better who Jesus is, is to take more account of not only the deity of Christ—which we must account for—but also, the humanity of Christ. Many of us have thought of Christ almost exclusively through the lens of deity. That's why we don't marvel at His obedience. We don't marvel at His resisting temptation. We think, *of course, He's God.* It's just automatic, right?

The New Testament clearly points to a different way of understanding how Jesus lived His life. Listen to Acts 10:38. In bringing the Gospel to the Gentiles, Peter tells Cornelius, "[You've heard] how God anointed Jesus of Nazareth with the Holy Spirit and with power. He went about doing good and healing all who were oppressed by the devil, for God was with him." Peter knows Jesus is God. He worshipped Jesus. He was with Thomas on that great day after the resurrection, when Jesus appeared in the room and said, "Thomas, come. Touch my side, my hands. Be not disbelieving but believe." And Thomas declared, "My Lord and my God" (John 20:28). He knows Jesus is God. But if you asked Peter the question, "How did He live His life, day by day? How did He perform His miracles? How did He render his obedience? How did He resist temptation?" He would answer, "He was a man, living our lives; the Second Adam, but living that life in the power of the

Spirit. So He can be for us an example for how we should live." We need to grow in our understanding of Christ as the God-man.

THE SPIRIT—Many conservative evangelicals have thrown the baby out with the bathwater—the baby being the Holy Spirit. Because of all things Pentecostal, Charismatic, and Third Wave, we have feared the excesses, and so we are hands-off when it comes to the Holy Spirit. But this is to our disadvantage. Why else would Jesus say in John 16:7, "It is to your advantage that I go away"? Think how those words would land on His hearers' ears! They had waited hundreds of years for a Messiah to come. How could it be to their advantage that this long-awaited Messiah would leave? Jesus says, "for if I do not go away, the Helper will not come to you. But if I go, I will send him to you."

What could be better than having Jesus walking by your side? Having the Spirit of Jesus living within your very life, empowering you for Christ-like transformation. The empowerment for everything we are called to be and to do is by the power of the Spirit. May God help us to see this.

SALVATION—A deeper understanding of salvation must begin with the doctrine of election. "Blessed be the God and Father of our Lord Jesus Christ, who has blessed us in Christ with every spiritual blessing in the heavenly places, even as he chose us in him before the foundation of the world, that we should be holy and blameless before him. In love he predestined us for adoption to himself as sons through Jesus Christ, according to the purpose of his will, to the praise of his glorious grace, with which he has blessed us in the Beloved" (Ephesians 1:3-6).

That was the Apostle Paul's list of why God should be praised, and the very first thing off his pen is, "He chose us." If you passed out a sheet of paper to people in an adult Sunday school class in churches across America and asked them to write the blessings of God, do you think election would be on the list? Would it top the list? Why does it top the list for the Apostle Paul? Because He knows that in eternity past the decision of God to have a chosen people put everything else in motion. Everything depends upon the fact that God chose to save;

to bring to Himself those who would be holy and blameless in the end only through the work of His Son.

Notice Ephesians 1:4 says that the Father chose us to be "holy and blameless." And Ephesians 5:27 says that Christ gave himself up for us in order to make us "holy and without blemish." How beautiful. What the Father ordains us to be, the Son accomplishes by His work on the cross. Starting with election, the whole of our salvation depends upon a gracious God who chooses to save those who do not deserve that salvation. So election should never promote within us an arrogance. God forbid! It should rather promote within us an intense humility and an incredible sense of privilege that God has shown His favor—can you believe it?—to us.

Everything that happens in salvation is grace upon grace upon grace. May God help us to see this.

CONSUMMATION—The doctrines of heaven and hell and the final judgment that will take place ought to be at the forefront of our thinking much more than they are. These are in the apostles' teaching. Do you know this? They are part of the evangelistic preaching of the book of Acts, that God has appointed a man, Jesus, by whom this judgment will take place. It should sober us to realize the everlasting reality of hell. And it ought to strengthen us to realize heaven is our true home. If you are in Christ, you are seated with Christ in the heavenlies. You are citizens of His Kingdom, and we wait for our King to come. May God help us to embrace the glory of what is ours, regardless of what happens in this age.

APPLYING LEARNING TO LIFE

In conclusion, take each of the items under breadth and depth and ask these three questions:

1. How can I grow in my understanding in each of these areas? What are some steps, even small steps, I can take? Little steps move you forward! The problem is taking no steps at all.

2. How can my affections be more stirred and more shaped by the weight and the glory of what each truth provides? God intends truth that He gives us to travel from our heads into our hearts and, only then, out through our hands in the way we live. We can't bypass the heart. God intends our hearts to be moved. He wants us not only to know the truth as truth; He wants us also to know the truth as beautiful, glorious, and weighty.

3. How can I be used in the lives of those of the next generation to commend to them—their heads and their hearts—the fullness of the whole counsel of God? How can I be used in their lives to help unpack the breadth of the whole counsel of God and the depth of the whole counsel of God?

May God help us not only to grow ourselves, but also be increasingly useful instruments in God's hands for shaping young lives to become what God wants them to be.

BRUCE A. WARE is Professor of Christian Theology at The Southern Baptist Theological Seminary. He and his wife, Jodi, have two grown daughters and three grandchildren.

5

Teaching the Difficult and Complex Doctrines to Children

The conviction and confidence
to teach what's hard

SALLY MICHAEL

...when all Israel comes to appear before the LORD your God at the place that he will choose, you shall read this law before all Israel in their hearing. Assemble the people, men, women, and little ones, and the sojourner within your towns, that they may hear and learn to fear the LORD your God, and be careful to do all the words of this law (Deuteronomy 31:11-12).

ASSEMBLE THE MEN, women...and little ones? To hear the law? Moses surely didn't know much about pedagogy...or did he? In the centuries that have passed since Moses gave this instruction, we have often departed from giving children the whole counsel of God, in favor of "bits and pieces" they can "understand." How often have we neglected deep truth and biblical doctrine in favor of imparting simple stories they can enjoy? Have we lost the benefits of what Tedd and Margy Tripp recommend when they write, "We give our children big truths they will grow into rather than light explanations they will grow out of"?[1]

These "big truths" are those truths that are often perceived as "too difficult" for children to understand, as well as those that may seem inappropriate for children—the ones that could generate fear, anxiety, or sadness. It is through these big truths—the breadth of biblical teaching from Genesis to Revelation—that the Holy Spirit works to convict their hearts and lead them to salvation.

REASONS FOR TEACHING THE DIFFICULT AND COMPLEX DOCTRINES TO CHILDREN

John Piper explains the overarching reason to teach doctrine to children:

> Sometimes it is necessary to stress that Christianity is primarily a relationship with Jesus rather than a set of ideas about Jesus. The reason we do this is because no one is saved by believing a set of ideas. The devil believes most of the truths of Christianity. We need to stress that unless a person has a living trust in Jesus as Savior and Lord, all the orthodoxy in the world will not get him into heaven.

> But if our stress on the personal relationship with Jesus leads us to deny that there is a set of truths essential to Christianity, we make a grave mistake. There are truths about God and Christ and man and the church and the world that are essential to the life of Christianity. If they are lost or distorted, the result will not be merely wrong ideas but misplaced trust. The inner life of faith is not independent from the doctrinal statement of faith. When doctrine goes bad, so do hearts. There is a body of doctrine that must be preserved.[2]

---

[1] Tedd and Margy Tripp book. *Instructing a Child's Heart* (Wapwallopen, Pa.: Shepherd Pr., 2008), 45.

[2] John Piper, "Contend for the Faith," Sermon preached at Bethlehem Church (Minneapolis, MN, November 25, 1984), https://www.desiringgod.org/messages/contend-for-the-faith

Though it is pedagogically controversial and countercultural, there are good reasons to teach children the breadth and depth of the Bible. Here are 13 of them.

1. IT GIVES CHILDREN AN ACCURATE VIEW OF GOD AND THE MESSAGE OF THE BIBLE. You would have a negative impression of a father forcefully pushing his child at the beach if that is all you saw. But if you saw the broken glass bottle the child almost stepped on, you would have a different impression of the scene. Seeing the whole picture, rather than just one aspect, makes the difference.

The same is true of God and the message of the Bible. If we over-emphasize one aspect of God's character or one doctrine of the Bible while minimizing or neglecting others, we will have a distorted picture of who God is and a skewed understanding of biblical truth. Over-emphasizing the law without an equally adequate understanding of grace can produce the notion that salvation is earned by good works. In contrast, emphasizing the grace of God to the exclusion of the justice of God can leave the impression that God in His goodness saves everyone. Both of these dangerously wrong conclusions are the result of unbalanced or incomplete teaching.

2. IT ENCOURAGES CHILDREN TO EMBRACE THE GOSPEL. 1 Peter 1:23 says that we are born again through the living and abiding Word of God. For spiritual transformation to occur, there must be an understanding of the message of redemption. Truly, grace makes no sense if sin is not understood; and sin is not understood apart from an understanding of the holiness of God. Although a complete understanding of the message of the Bible is not needed for a child to respond in sincere faith, there has to be an adequate understanding.

3. CHILDREN ARE NOT HINDERED IN THEIR ACCEPTANCE OF HARD TRUTHS BY PAST EXPERIENCES, EMOTIONS, OR PREJUDICES. Children are usually very black and white in their thinking, and without "emotional baggage" to cloud their thinking, they more readily accept hard truths than adults do. Suffering is not personal to most children; it is theoretical. Usually, they easily understand and accept God's judgment and His sovereignty over all things, including evil. Establishing a theological framework for children gives them a biblical perspective that informs their hearts and helps them to interpret their life experiences correctly. Without this framework to inform their experience, their experience will drive their biblical understanding.

4. CHILDREN'S HEARTS ARE TYPICALLY TENDER TOWARD TRUTH, AND THEREFORE IT IS CRITICAL TO TEACH TRUTH TO THEM BEFORE THEIR HEARTS ARE HARDENED. We have a window of opportunity to cooperate with the work of the Holy Spirit through the Word of God to incline the open hearts of children toward Jesus. Paul's admonition to Timothy is a good word to us as we teach the next generation:

> preach the word; be ready in season and out of season; reprove, rebuke, and exhort, with complete patience and teaching. For the time is coming when people will not endure sound teaching, but having itching ears they will accumulate for themselves teachers to suit their own passions, and will turn away from listening to the truth and wander off into myths (2 Timothy 4:2-4).

We must be ready at all times to patiently teach the full counsel of God while children's hearts are tender because the time is coming when they will "not endure sound teaching" but will be swayed by the false philosophies of this world. It is easier to mold a tender heart than a calloused heart. This tenderness is a gift from God to be appreciated, and should motivate us to diligently sow as much as we can of the precious truths of who God is and how He works in the world and in the hearts of men.

5. KNOWING THE WORD IS THE FOUNDATION FOR FEARING GOD AND PROTECTION FROM SIN. It is impossible to fear God without knowing who He is, or to love the truth unless the truth is known. The following verses clearly teach that

knowing the truth lays a foundation for a fear of the Lord and righteous living:

> The fear of the LORD is the beginning of wisdom, and the knowledge of the Holy One is insight (Proverbs 9:10).

> I have stored up your word in my heart, that I might not sin against you (Psalm 119:11).

6. THE TRUTH IS LEARNED PRECEPT UPON PRECEPT. Children, as all of us, learn by building upon prior knowledge (Isaiah 28:9-13). Layer upon layer of teaching adds more understanding. When we present the full counsel of God to a child, the child absorbs what he can, not only when he hears the teaching but even later as he reflects when it comes to mind. Each successive teaching of that truth gives the child a broader and a deeper understanding as God's Word does its effectual work:

> The unfolding of your words gives light; it imparts understanding to the simple (Psalm 119:130).

7. IT GIVES CHILDREN A BIBLICAL FRAMEWORK FROM WHICH TO INTERPRET ALL OF LIFE. We are all interpreters of our experience. We will either wrongly interpret that experience according to human wisdom, or by God's grace, interpret it rightly through an understanding of the Bible. If children are given a biblical framework from which to interpret all of life, they will have a more correct understanding of life. Correctly responding to life comes first through correctly understanding it.

For example, I had planned a class field trip to the zoo but had to cancel it due to rain. Some of the children were upset, but I had one four-year-old boy in my class who said simply, "Teacher, God probably looked down and saw a little flower that needed to be watered and sent the rain." His theology informed his childlike understanding of his experience. He believed in God's sovereign providence over all creation, and though disappointed, he was able to embrace that God had other good purposes.

8. BEING TAUGHT THE WHOLE COUNSEL OF GOD HELPS PREVENT WRONG THINKING THAT MUST BE UNDONE LATER IN LIFE. Have you ever tried to teach a child to hold a pencil correctly, after years of holding it incorrectly? If so, you know it is easier to correctly teach something from the outset than to retrain a bad habit or understanding. It is no different with bad theology. In the 1980s, David and I sat under the preaching of John Piper every Sunday as he labored to correct the wrong theology of the adults in the sanctuary. Meanwhile, the same wrong theology was being taught upstairs the following hour to our children. So when we were called to lead children's ministry, we determined to teach children accurate theology from the youngest ages. We had seen too many adults endure faith crises in the midst of trials because they had never had a theology of suffering. It can be faith shattering to have your misunderstanding of God and the Bible corrected as an adult.

We want to begin putting rocks of solid doctrine under the feet of our children right from the start. We have a great God. He is a rock we can stand on when everything else is shaking. The winds of adversity will blow on our children. How much better to prepare them when they are young with the understanding that, "When you pass through the waters, I will be with you; and through the rivers, they shall not overwhelm you..." (Isaiah 43:2a), than with the false notion that Jesus called the disciples because He "needed helpers." A God who needs us to help Him is a weak God indeed, not a Rock to stand on.

9. SOLID TEACHING ENCOURAGES CHILDREN TO BECOME MATURE IN THEIR FAITH. Though initially we must introduce children to the simple truths of the Bible, we must progress beyond a continual diet of simplistic truths if we expect children to grow to maturity.

> For though by this time you ought to be teachers, you need someone to teach you again the basic principles of the oracles of God. You need milk, not solid food, for everyone who lives on milk is unskilled in the word of righteousness, since he is a child. But solid food is for

the mature, for those who have their powers of discernment trained by constant practice to distinguish good from evil (Hebrews 5:12-14).

If we want children to become mature in faith, we must give them "solid food."

Young children can understand big truths like the sovereignty of God and the omniscience of God; that God is incomprehensible, self-existent, self-sufficient, and eternal; that God is three-in-one; and He is a jealous God. They can learn big words like regeneration, justification, and sanctification and understand their definitions and what the Bible teaches about them. If they are explained carefully and age-appropriately, these truths are not too mature for children. The Holy Spirit can give children an understanding of spiritual matters beyond their capacity. The Holy Spirit does not work in a vacuum, however, but through the inspired Word of God diligently taught.

While telling the story of Shadrach, Meshach, and Abednego, one of our Sunday school teachers asked the class, "Should they bow down to Nebuchadnezzar's golden statue?" One little girl got very agitated, started waving her hand, and blurted out, "They can't. They can't, because of that verse." She pointed to the wall where the symbols for the verse cards were hung. The verse she was pointing to? "No one can serve two masters" (Matthew 6:24a).

The little girl who said it was only three years old. That's a big conviction for such a small person. But she has a big God who faithfully connected the truth of a verse she learned in the church nursery to a Bible story she was hearing as a preschooler.

Children can learn big truths like the sovereignty and omniscience of God; that God is incomprehensible, self-existent, self-sufficient, and eternal; that God is three-in-one and He is a jealous God. Their active minds can grasp significant truths like regeneration, justification, and sanctification if they are explained appropriately.

10. DISCERNMENT IS TRAINED THROUGH CONSTANT PRACTICE. The same tenderness of heart that inclines children toward the truth—coupled with the gullibility or innocence of youth, and the ready trust of others—can render children vulnerable to deception. Each day children are bombarded with godless perspectives and false philosophies that permeate the air they breathe. How can we protect them from the lies of the enemy?

Experts at identifying counterfeit money are trained by careful scrutiny of real bills. If the characteristics of genuine bills is engrained in their minds, they can spot forgeries. The best defense our children have against falling prey to untruth is a robust knowledge of the truth.

Scripture says, "In Christ...are hidden all the treasures of wisdom and knowledge" (see Colossians 2:1-8). John McArthur says, "Knowing and understanding the Word of righteousness—taking in solid food—trains your senses to discern good and evil."[3] Our children must have a storehouse of truth, of memorized verses and biblical understanding, to discern truth from error. But discernment is often misunderstood. "Discernment results from a carefully disciplined mind. It is not a matter of feelings, nor is discernment a mystical gift,"[4] says McArthur. The greatest weapon our children have against lies is the truth as revealed in the full counsel of God from Genesis to Revelation. The Apostle Paul says that discernment is a matter of training (Hebrews 5:14), which involves more than just a cursory knowledge of the Bible but a precept-upon-precept foundation of truth.

11. CHILDREN CAN ONLY SEE THEMSELVES ACCURATELY AS THEY LOOK INTO THE WORD OF GOD. Children are naturally self-righteous. Seeing themselves as "good," they don't realize that they are in desperate need of rescue from their sin nature and the resulting condemnation. Without an understanding of the holiness of God and His righteous demands, they cannot see themselves as sinful. But as they see Israel's apostasy in story after story in the Old Testament, they begin to realize man's utter failure to trust and obey God...and they get a glimpse into the true condition of the sinful human heart. As the doctrine of God, man, sin, and salvation are uncovered throughout the Bible, they can begin to understand

---

[3] John McArthur, *The Truth War* (Nashville, TN: Thomas Nelson, 2007), 213.
[4] McArthur, 214.

the condition of the human heart and the only remedy for sinners—including themselves.

As they see God's character on display in the Old and New Testament, the constancy of His presence; the strength of His power over flood, hail, the sun, and the wind and waves; and the sureness of His control to bring all circumstances to His determined end, they begin to glimpse the centrality of God. As they look into the Holy Scripture, they begin to understand that all of life revolves around God...that He is the center of the universe and not themselves.

12. THE WORD EVOKES WORSHIP IN THOSE WHO HAVE EYES TO SEE ITS GLORIOUS TRUTHS. For those who have eyes to see God in His manifold excellencies, the involuntary response is awe. For example, when our eyes are opened to God's grace to choose sinners to become saints, before the foundation of the world, in spite of our utter inability to respond without His grace—we can't help worship. When we deny children this and other glorious truths, we stifle their worship.

13. SO WE WILL STAND IN THE JUDGMENT AS GOOD SHEPHERDS. Paul said to the elders at Ephesus:

> "You yourselves know how I lived among you the whole time from the first day that I set foot in Asia, serving the Lord with all humility and with tears and with trials that happened to me through the plots of the Jews; how I did not shrink from declaring to you anything that was profitable, and teaching you in public and from house to house, testifying both to Jews and to Greeks of repentance toward God and of faith in our Lord Jesus Christ....(Acts 20:18-21)...Therefore I testify to you this day that I am innocent of the blood of all of you, for I did not shrink from declaring to you the whole counsel of God (Acts 20:26-27).

We are responsible to teach those we shepherd, regardless of age, all that is "profitable" for them.

OBJECTIONS TO TEACHING DIFFICULT AND COMPLEX DOCTRINES TO CHILDREN

Not surprisingly, many people disagree with this approach to teaching children and raise the following objections:

THESE TRUTHS ARE INAPPROPRIATE TO TEACH TO CHILDREN.

Sitting through the previews of upcoming "children's movies" in a movie theater was eye opening for me. "Children's movie" after "children's movie" portrayed darkness, violence, evil, and deception. Children's videos and television shows aren't much different, glamorizing sin for the sake of entertainment. It is ironic that many parents fail to monitor their children's viewing choices, while objecting to teaching the hard truths of the Bible. The Bible does not shield us from the unpleasant and the ugly.

The Bible is full of "inappropriate truth"—two daughters who plot to get pregnant by their father; a brother who pretends to be sick and violates his sister; a king who commits adultery and then murder; a woman who drives a tent peg through a man's head; a seductive young woman who dances before her drunken stepfather and his drunken friends and demands the head of a prophet on a platter...and a Savior nailed to a cross. The Bible does not shield us from the unpleasant and the ugly. It is a true portrayal of mankind. Unlike Hollywood, the Bible presents these realities appropriately, without unnecessary detail, and with the aim of evoking a correct heart response. We can do the same...and tell a preschooler that David stole another man's wife and treated her like his own wife.

Some object to teaching children about sin and hell in an effort to avoid making children scared or uncomfortable. But why would we want to "protect" our children from the very truths that can lead them to salvation? John Piper says, "...if we don't know what our real plight is, we may not recognize God's rescue when it comes." Similarly, Randy Alcorn says, "Fear of Hell serves as a merciful call to repentance."

It is less important that our children "feel comfortable" than that they feel convicted.

THESE TRUTHS ARE TOO HARD FOR CHILDREN TO UNDERSTAND.

It may take some thoughtfulness and creativity to bring

profound truths to a child's level, but God can enable us to communicate His big truths to young children. A young child may not grasp the meaning of the providence of God through memorizing the Westminister Catechism definition of providence. But explaining God's providence using the image of an eye and a hand can bring it to down to their level: The providence of God means that God's eye is watching over the universe and God's hand is at work in the universe. I would hasten to add that memorizing a catechism definition, though not fully comprehensible to a young child, is a truth he will grow into; one that will provide a sound theological foundation.

THESE TRUTHS ARE TOO HARD FOR ADULTS TO UNDERSTAND, SO WE CAN'T TEACH THEM TO CHILDREN. Many of us were not well-taught when we were young in the faith. When we hear theological terms we may have a vague sense of what they mean, though it only takes a couple of probing questions for us to realize how little we actually understand. However, lack of understanding is not a good reason to keep truth from our children, and it is something we can remedy. Truth78 curriculum is designed to train teachers as well as children, and to fill in those theological cracks that are lacking in our education. By teaching precept upon precept, using concrete illustrations and explanations, and teaching the hard doctrines within the context of other doctrines, complex theological concepts can be taught simply to a child.

Though children will undoubtedly ask questions the teacher or parent cannot answer, no teacher or parent should feel the pressure to know all the answers. An honest, "I don't know, but I'll find out," allows you time to look for an answer.

CHILDREN WILL BE BORED WITH ALL OF THIS THEOLOGY. Anything we teach, even simple concepts, can be boring to children. And just about anything we teach can be interesting and even exciting for children to learn. Whether children are bored or interested depends more on how the material is taught and on the condition of the child's heart than on the subject matter itself. In other words, boredom is a problem of methods more than material, and of condition than content. The risk of boredom is not a reason for keeping truth from our children. Instead, this risk should challenge us to overcome every obstacle that keeps children from hearing and loving the truth.

THESE TOPICS ARE TOO CONTROVERSIAL. I will get in trouble if I teach these things. Most topics are not controversial. For those that are, the wise course of action is just to stick to the biblical texts, and be winsome rather than argumentative. If our source is the Bible itself, the only controversy a person can have is with God. At that point, our responsibility is to pray that God will open that person's eyes and heart. We must not negate our responsibility to teach the whole counsel of God, even if some people don't understand or agree, regardless of the consequences.

HOW TO TEACH DIFFICULT AND COMPLEX DOCTRINES TO CHILDREN

INTRODUCE BASIC CONCEPTS EARLY. Young children can understand complex theology if it is taught simply in age-appropriate language and connected to something they experience in their own lives. It requires thoughtfulness and preparation to bring difficult or complex theology to little children, but with practice it is possible.

For example, the sovereignty of God can be taught to preschoolers using the simple language and life connection that "God is the boss of all things." A small child can understand the explanation that daddy is the boss of the family. Mommy is the boss when daddy isn't home. Daddy has a boss at work who decides when daddy will work and how much daddy will get paid and if daddy can take a vacation. But God is the boss of everyone and everything—He is the boss of the stars, and the flowers and the snow and sickness—and God is the boss of mommy and daddy and the president—and God is the boss of me.

Connecting the real-life example to Bible stories puts content, context, and richness to the child's understanding. For example, a preschooler can understand that as the boss, God is in charge of all things. He is in charge of the wind and the waves—like when Jesus stopped the storm. He is in charge of the armies of Israel and the enemies of Israel, and He sent hail to stop the enemy soldiers. God is in charge of sickness—so Jesus told the man whose legs didn't work to get up and walk—and he did. God is in charge of the mouths of lions, and He shut the lions' mouths so Daniel would not get hurt.

TEACH PRECEPT UPON PRECEPT. Children can't always see the "big picture." Biblical truths can look more like a dot-to-dot picture to them, a smattering of unconnected knowledge. But starting with simple explanations at a young age, little by little we can begin to connect the dots until the big picture becomes understandable. Teaching precept upon precept is intentional; it is purposeful. It involves teaching terminology, verses, stories, principles, and concepts—and then step-by-step filling that knowledge with meaning.

How does a child understand the meaning of any big concept? We break it down for them. A baby doesn't understand that a stove gets very hot and can burn you. But a baby can understand the meaning of the word "no" when he reaches his hand out toward the frying pan. When he is a toddler, he can understand that he must sit down at the other side of the kitchen when mommy opens the oven because he might get hurt. An elementary-aged child, under mommy's watchful eye, can take something out of the oven with potholders. He has learned that the potholders will protect his hands from the heat. And a 12-year-old can be responsible enough to bake brownies by himself. All those concepts were learned precept upon precept.

Biblical truths are taught in much the same manner. At the preschool level, we can teach all the major doctrines of the Bible stated as simple truths in simple language...and from that we progress to greater depth and scope.

Example: The doctrine of sin.

Toddler: "We do bad things."
Preschooler: "We have bad hearts that make us do bad things. We disobey God. We need new hearts."
Early elementary: "Sin is disobeying God. We think, feel, and do bad things because we have sinful hearts. Everyone was born a sinner and only Jesus can give us new hearts." (We would also teach about the

holiness of God and eventually contrast sinful man to a Holy God.)
Later elementary: "God is holy and righteous (perfect in every way).
God made us to be like Him so we must be holy and righteous—obeying
His commands, perfectly all the time. We are not holy and righteous;
we were born sinful and have a sin nature. As sinners we have sinful
hearts that think, feel, and do sinful things that offend God, and our
disobedience to God must be punished.

USE CONCRETE ILLUSTRATIONS AND EXPLANATIONS.
Jesus often taught by way of illustration, using concrete objects or
situations in the real world to explain spiritual truth. He instructed
us not to worry by pointing out God's care for birds and lilies;
He compared the impossibility of a rich man to enter heaven to
a camel going through the eye of a needle; and He compared the
Kingdom of heaven to a treasure in a field. He taught through
story using parables to help those with eyes to see and understand
spiritual truths.

God has given us the same rich context in which to teach children. His whole creation provides examples for us to bridge the gap
between the concrete and the spiritual.

Example: God's holiness and the necessary separation of sinful man
from a Holy God.

(Show a clean white shirt.) Would you put this shirt in a toolbox? Why
not? Would you want this shirt to be anywhere near the tool box?
Would the owner of this shirt allow you to stuff the shirt in a toolbox
and get grease on it?

God is like the white shirt. He is so pure and spotless and good that
we cannot bring sin near Him. We cannot come into His presence as
sinful people.

RELATE BIBLICAL DOCTRINE TO REAL LIFE. Bible doctrine
is not divorced from real life; it is not something we assign to classroom teaching or family devotions. It is to be woven into everyday

life as Deuteronomy 6:4-7 instructs us, talking of them as we sit in our houses, walk by the way, when we lie down, and when we rise.

> **Example:** A new child joins your Sunday school class. By commenting, "I'm so glad God brought you to our class," you have interpreted that life experience for the children through the lens of the sovereignty of God. It was not chance that brought the child to the class, but God who orchestrates all things.

TEACH THE HARD DOCTRINES IN THE CONTEXT OF OTHER BIBLE DOCTRINES. Teaching about hell should be balanced by teaching about heaven; sin should be accompanied by redemption; and the wrath of God should be set in the context of the mercy of God—all of these doctrines should be part of the scope taught to children. Doctrines should not be taught in isolation but placed within the framework of the whole counsel of God.

> **Example:** A child being treated meanly by another child.

> "I am sorry Larry treated you so poorly. That was wrong—it was sinful. That sin hurt Larry; it hurt you; and most of all, it grieved God who hates sin.

> "It is hard for us when we are treated so unkindly. I wonder if that is how Joseph felt when his brothers threw him into the pit—or when Potiphar's wife lied about him and Potiphar threw him in jail. What do you think?

> "Do you know that it is not so important what that person did. It is more important what God is doing. Do you remember what Joseph said to his brothers when they realized who he was? Yes, he said, 'You meant it for evil but God meant it for good.'

> "When other people treat us unkindly, we need to remember that even though they have unkindness in their hearts, God—who does not stop them from doing that bad thing—has only love in His heart

for us. He always has a good reason for doing what He does. What good things do you think God could be doing through this unkindness?"

In this example, the adult has helped the child to interpret this life experience biblically. He has been show the reality of the ugliness of sin; he has been helped to see that suffering is part of the human experience; this bad experience has been placed within the context of God's sovereign hand; the wisdom of God has been commended the wisdom of God.

The Bible is full of multifaceted truth. It is rich in its teaching about God and His involvement with His world and with man. Though suffering is a reality, so is the glorious truth that the day is coming when there will be no more suffering…and teaching these two truths in tandem spans the breadth of biblical teaching on suffering and provides balance.

SOW THE SEED AND TRUST GOD FOR THE GROWTH. The Bible is a coherent whole, wonderfully complex, and wonderfully simple at the same time. It is easy enough for children to comprehend, and yet incomprehensible to the most astute thinkers. It is the inspired Word of God; powerful to bring about salvation as it displays the wonder of our great God and His multifaceted character.

We have been given the astounding privilege of instructing the next generation in the glorious truths of the Bible and to introducing them to Jesus. Matt and Elizabeth Schmucker wisely exhort parents to "Pack in truth while your children are little and trust the Lord to unpack it in his time." Though children won't immediately, fully understand the richness of what we are teaching them, neither have we plumbed the depths of the mysteries of God. We "see in part" as we mine the treasures of His Word. So too children. The Holy Spirit will bring understanding in His time. It is our task to faithfully teach the fullness of biblical truth.

SALLY MICHAEL is the co-founder of Truth78 and co-author of the curriculum, devotionals, and books. She and her husband, David, have two grown daughters and three grandchildren.

6

Parents, the Primary Disciplers of Their Children

*You can't give your children
what you don't have*

TIMOTHY PAUL JONES

THE ANIMATED FEATURE *The Incredibles* is a favorite movie in our household—and one of my favorite scenes is the family meal early in the film. Dinner at the Parr household has deteriorated into sheer pandemonium. The infant squeals in delight at the chaos as his two siblings engage in super-powered combat with each other. A frazzled mom stretches and strains unsuccessfully to restore order.

And what about Bob Parr, father and former "Mr. Incredible"? He stands to the side, physically present, relationally absent, and utterly uncertain as to what to do. His sole advice thus far has been, "Kids, listen to your mother."

Finally, his wife flings a frantic plea in his direction: "Bob! It's time to engage! Don't just stand there. Do something!" And, to his credit, Bob Parr does try. The problem is, Mr. Incredible has no clue how to engage the situation wisely, and his engagement results in greater chaos.

Then, the doorbell rings. Suddenly, everyone scrambles for a seat at the table and, by the time the door opens, what the visitor sees is a perfectly placid all-American family.

Many parents in your congregation have been walking in Mr. Incredible's shoes for a long time. They have observed their children's spiritual development from a disengaged distance. They have watched youth and children's ministers stretch and strain to promote growth. And though we as youth ministers and children's directors have tried to hide it from them, most of these parents have noticed that we don't have it all together. Still, they're watching, wondering if they should play a larger part in the discipleship of their families.

Now, in a growing movement in churches throughout the world, ministers are suddenly turning to these parents and shouting, "It's time to engage!"

But how?

THE HOME AS FOUNDATION FOR DISCIPLESHIP: BIBLICAL FOUNDATIONS FOR FAMILY MINISTRY

In some cases, parents seem to think that the church bears sole responsibility for their children's spiritual formation—and, to be fair, that's precisely the impression that church leaders have sometimes given to parents. Whether or not we intended to do so, we've focused so heavily on age-organized programs that it seems as if parents can simply plug their child into church programs from birth to high school graduation and the child will become a fully mature Christian adult. But that's not what Scripture tells us. God's Word makes it clear that parents have a necessary role in the discipleship of their children (Deuteronomy 6:4; Ephesians 5:32-33; 6:1-4). In addition to this role, the church as the family of God has the responsibility to disciple spiritual orphans—children in the church whose parents are not believers.

In a world that organizes itself into groupings that are based on age and interest, it is radically cultural to expect parents to disciple their children and church members to build relationships that transcend generational divisions. And yet, when we remain separated from one another, we can easily develop cultures where the lives of those who are younger and those who are older never intersect. But that's not God's design. God longs to turn the generations toward one another instead of away from one another (Malachi 4:6).

Discipleship at home is particularly crucial in this regard because what you do for God beyond your home will typically never be greater than what you practice with God within your home. The home, Martin Luther said, is a "school for character." If we want the hearts of the generations to be turned toward one another at church, those habits must begin in the home. If we want people to make disciples of all nations, we must begin by training parents to disciple the children in their homes. If we want the people in our church to be evangelists, we must begin by training fathers and mothers to lead their own children to profess faith in Jesus Christ. If we want church members to handle conflict well within the church, we must teach them to deal with conflict effectively in their homes. If we want people to reach out to broken and hurting people outside the church, we must equip them to use their homes as contexts to care for spiritual orphans.

According to Paul, a candidate for pastor "must manage his own household well" (1 Timothy 3:4). And what is Paul's rationale for such a requirement? "If anyone does not know how to manage his own household, how will he care for God's church?" (1 Timothy 3:5). How you live at home shapes how you act in the church. What you do within your home prepares you for what God calls you to do beyond your home, and what you do for God beyond your home will rarely be greater than what you're practicing with God within your home.

TRAIN YOUR CHILDREN IN THE FEAR OF GOD: HISTORICAL FOUNDATIONS FOR FAMILY MINISTRY

Even in the earliest stages of Christian history, church leaders understood the importance of parental discipleship. Near the end of the first century, Clement of Rome admonished parents in his congregation, "Let our children receive the instruction that is in the Messiah. Let our children receive the instruction that is in the Messiah. Let them learn...how the fear of God is good and great and saves all those who live in this fear in holiness with a pure mind."[1]

The *Shepherd,* written by a man named Hermas, was a very popular text among second-century Christians. It seems clear from this writing that parental discipline and discipleship of children was a challenge even in the second century. Here's how the angelic messenger depicted in this book admonished the father who received the visions:

> Convert your family, which has sinned against the Lord and against you. You are so fond of your children that you have not corrected your family, but instead allowed them to become terribly corrupt! This is why the Lord is angry with you. But he will heal all your past deeds that have been done by your family.[2]

In the fourth century, John Chrysostom preached a sermon in which he declared,

> To each of the fathers and mothers I speak. Just as we see artists fashioning their paintings and statues with great precision, so we must care for these wondrous statues of ours. Painters, once they've set the canvas on the easel, paint on it day by day to fulfill their purpose. Sculptors working in marble precede in a similar manner. They remove what is unhelpful and they add what is lacking. You should proceed in the same way. Like the creators of statues, give your leisure time to fashioning these wonderful statues of God. Remove what is unhelpful, add what is lacking. Inspect them day by day to see what good qualities nature has supplied so that you can increase these qualities and see which faults you can eradicate in them....Make them athletes for Christ.[3]

What a challenge for contemporary parents! Developing our children as athletes in sports or as students in particular school subjects

---

[1] Translated from 1 *Clement* 21.8, in *The Apostolic Fathers,* vol. 1, ed. And trans. Bart D. Ehrman, Loeb Classical
[2] Shepherd of Hermas, *Vision,* 1.3.1.
[3] John Chrysostom, *De Inani,* 19, 39, 63, 90.

isn't wrong—but it is far more important to train them to be, in Chrysostom's words, "athletes for Christ."
More than a millennium after Chrysostom, Martin Luther suggested,

> If we would reinstate Christianity into its former glory, we must improve and elevate the children, as it was done in the days of old.... Wherefore it is the chief duty of the father of the family to bestow greater, more constant care upon the soul of his child than upon his own body, for this is his own flesh, but the soul of the child is a precious jewel that God has entrusted to his keeping.[4]

Writing in the 17th century, Richard Baxter recommended to pastors,

> Get the masters of families to do their duty, and they will not only spare you a great deal of labor, but will much further the success of your labors. You are not likely to see any general reformation till you procure family reformation. Some little religion there may be here and there, but while it is confined to single persons and is not promoted in families, it will not prosper nor promise much future increase.[5]

After undergoing a forcible termination at Northampton Congregational Church, Jonathan Edwards included the following words in his farewell sermon:

> Every Christian family ought to be, as it were, a little church—wholly governed, consecrated to Christ, wholly governed and influenced by his rules and family education and order are some of the chief means of grace. If these are duly maintained, all the means of grace will be likely to prosper and to be successful.[6]

---

[4] Karl Von Raumer, "Luther's Views of Education and Schools," *The American Journal of Education,* vol. 4, 1857, 425.
[5] Richard Baxter, *The Reformed Pastor* (Glasgow, Scotland: W. Collins & Co.), 88. books.google.com
[6] Jonathan Edwards, *Selected Writings of Jonathan Edwards, Second Edition* with introduction and afterword by Harold P. Simonson (Long Grove, Illinois: Waveland Press, Inc.) 116.

THE IMPACT OF PARENTAL FAITH: SOCIAL-SCIENTIFIC SUPPORT FOR FAMILY MINISTRY

The authoritative witness of Scripture and the supportive witness of church history testify together that parents have a necessary role when it comes to the discipleship of their children. Social-scientific research supports this supposition as well. Sociologist Christian Smith points out in his book *Soul Searching* that the beliefs of teenagers seldom vary significantly from the beliefs of their parents. Only 11% say their religious beliefs are very different from their fathers' and only 6% very different from their mothers.[7]

And yet, according to the research that I completed while writing the book *Family Ministry Field Guide,* nearly half of church-involved parents have disengaged from the discipleship of their children. The vast majority of Christian parents affirm that they are responsible to disciple their children, but a large percentage have nevertheless disengaged from their children's spiritual formation. Of those who have disengaged from discipling their children, about 90% identified one or both of the following two issues as the roadblocks that prevented discipleship in their households: (1) I don't know how, and, (2) I don't have time.

It is imperative that churches help parents to receive the training they need and make the time to disciple their children. According to pollster George Barna:

> no matter how hard a church tries, it is incapable of bringing a child to complete spiritual maturity....Teenagers rarely embrace Christianity if their family has treated faith as a Sunday morning experience... the family...must have worship experiences, pray together about significant personal needs, study the meaning of Scriptures together, and serve others.[8]

So how are churches doing when it comes to training parents for this task? According to research undertaken for the book *Family Ministry Field Guide* as well as a survey from FamilyLife, about 80 percent

---

[7] Christian Smith, *Soul Searching* (New York, NY: Oxford University Press, 2009) 34.

[8] George Barna, *Real Teens* (Ventura, CA: Regal Books, 2001) 149.

of churched parents have never received guidance or training from their churches when it comes to the discipleship of their children.[9]

THE COUNTERCULTURAL HABITS OF FAMILY DISCIPLESHIP

God created and designed the family to be the primary context for human development, and male and female to be the primary distinction among persons. In the new covenant, God has formed the church to be a multigenerational, multiethnic community that serves as a family for those who are in Christ Jesus. By contrast, our contemporary culture suggests that the primary context for human flourishing is homogeneous groups and that the primary distinction between persons is whatever they prefer. In too many instances, church structures and organizations have reflected the culture more than they have reflected God's design. As a result, we often don't know how to be with one another, we don't know how to be with our kids, we don't know how to be with ourselves, and we don't know how to be with God.

There are so many practices to which I could call churches and parents at this point—family devotional times, rites of passage, personal times of discipleship with our children, for example. And all of those are good! But I want to begin with three far simpler practices. These simpler practices are intended to provide the foundation for deeper practices of discipleship. These three practices are simply *being together, serving together,* and *celebrating together.*

BE TOGETHER

An article in *The Atlantic* entitled "The Importance of Eating Together" cites Harris Poll findings indicating that the majority of American families eat a meal together less than once every five days. Even when families are together, they are frequently distracted by smartphones or watching a television program. They may be together physically, but they remain separated relationally and conversationally. Moses described

---

[9] Timothy Paul Jones, *Family Ministry Field Guide* (Indianapolis, IN: Wesleyan Publishing House), 26, 218.

how the parents of Israel should talk about God's truth "when you sit in your house, and when you walk by the way, and when you lie down, and when you rise" (Deuteronomy 6:7). Such conversations emerge naturally in the context of spending undistracted time together. Make time to be together and, in those moments, look for ways to connect God's glory and God's story to the ordinary events of life.

Have you seen that child who walks into the restaurant with headphones on, plugged into a smartphone or a video game, and continues to focus on the device throughout the meal? Or what about the parent who is constantly checking email throughout the same meal? What are we implicitly declaring to one another through these habits? We are each saying that I have my own world and that my own world matters more than the people around me. Let's model better practices and teach our children to develop these better practices with us.

SERVE TOGETHER

I saw something beautiful not long ago while walking down Brecken-ridge Lane in Louisville. In a front yard not far from my home, a young mother was removing leaves from a flower bed—an ordinary activity in the middle of an ordinary day. What was extraordinary about this scene was what I saw beside her. A tow-haired boy, perhaps three or four years old, was attempting to assist her. His rake was man-sized, his movements were far from efficient, and he was leaving more leaves than he moved. And yet, as I passed this mother and child, I heard no criticisms of his inefficiency. Instead, I heard encouragement and equipping: "Daddy will be so proud of your hard work! Can you try to get those leaves over there?" she asked as she gestured toward a hard-to-reach corner. "You know, honey, it might work better if you turned the rake over."

If this young woman's sole goal for yesterday afternoon was leaf removal, her best bet would have been to plop her preschooler in front of a television to watch professionally-produced children's programs that pretend to equip children with skills for life. Then she could have pursued the goal of beautifying the flower bed far more efficiently.

This woman had a goal that was far bigger than any flower bed, though. She understood that her real purpose on this day was not to improve a yard but to shape a soul. She was teaching her child the value of work and partnership and family structures, in addition to which side of a rake is supposed to be turned toward the ground. She was an amateur, with no college-transcripted credentials in motherhood or leaf removal. But that was all for the best anyway because no professional program can develop in a child what this mother was engraving in her son's soul that afternoon.

Working together is a powerful gift, and what we learn by working together is far more important than the efficient completion of any task that may stand before us. And so, work together, not only at home but also at church. Your children will likely learn as much or more by serving alongside you at church as they will from any class the church may offer.

CELEBRATE TOGETHER

Entertainment in our culture has become increasingly individualized. In many families, this means everyone watches their own entertainment on their own devices. What happens as a result is that individualized entertainment replaces the celebration of community.

In our household, no one plays a video game or watches a movie or television show alone. When we purchase a video game, it must be a multiplayer game. If we buy a Blu-Ray or download a television program, it has to be something that several people want to watch. Why do I require this? It's because I want my children to associate entertainment not with personalized amusement but with the celebration of something together.

It's interesting to me that, in the Scriptures, it seems as if an individual celebration is an impossibility. That which entertains is to be experienced in community. I still happen to think that's a healthy structure for all of us.

As a family, work toward replacing the cheap thrill of personalized amusements with the lasting joy of celebration in community. As a church, look for ways that you can help people to engage in celebrations that transcend the generations. Have families compete against one another at church activities in ways that are focused on fun rather than winning. Look for ways to include older generations in these activities, engaging in ways that fit their physical capacities. Include singles and spiritual orphans to build relationships that are bigger than family units.

WHAT'S NEXT?

If you help families learn to be together, to serve together, and to celebrate together, learning together will come much more naturally to them. But you can't just hope this happens. You will still have to equip them to do this because parents are *responsible* to God to serve as disciple makers in their children's lives. To do this, they will need to be *trained*. For most of them, it's something they have never experienced. That's why they don't know how to disciple their own children. And so, equip parents to disciple their children in ways that are memorable, that are missional, that are multigenerational—in ways that call them to spiritual conversations, biblical teaching in the home, as well as family worship. By God's grace, we can break the cycle. Acknowledge parents as disciple makers in their child's lives, train them *how* to engage in discipleship in their children's lives, and lovingly hold them accountable.

If your sole goal is organizational efficiency as a church leader, constantly acknowledging the role of parents is probably an inefficient use of your time and turning over children's spiritual lives to professionals at church would make perfect sense. But efficiency is not the goal of Gospel-motivated ministry. The crucified and risen Lord Jesus determines the shape and establishes the goal for His church. And it is His Father's good pleasure to form the church as a conglomeration of amateurs, not as a corporation run by professionals (1 Corinthians 12:4-31). The Spirit does not give gifts for the purpose of making the church efficient; he arranges the gifts in the body according to His will to make us holy (1 Corinthians 12:11).

The role of God-called leaders in the church is to encourage, acknowledge, and equip fellow members of the church to serve as ministers and missionaries first within their own households, and then far beyond their households (Ephesians 4:11-13; Acts 2:39). These processes are not likely to be quick or efficient. Sometimes, it may feel as if professionalized programs to disciple children would be an easier solution, but no church program can develop in a child what parents are able to engrave in their children's souls day-by-day.

TIMOTHY PAUL JONES is Professor of Christian Family Ministry and Associate Vice President at The Southern Baptist Theological Seminary. He is married to Rayann, and they have four daughters.

7

Teaching the Essential Truths of the Gospel to Children

Are we building unshakable foundations?

JILL NELSON

MY FAMILY ENJOYS old-fashioned tent camping. We have a very large tent that my children affectionately call the "Taj Mahal." Assembling the tent involves the key components: fabric, metal poles, and ropes; and their proper assembly. For example, the poles must first be constructed and threaded through specific sleeves of the tent fabric. This takes time. There is no shortcut. But when every pole is properly in place, you simply pull on the guide ropes and the massive tent goes up and takes its proper shape.

This illustration can be helpful in demonstrating the importance of how we present the Gospel to our children and students. There is a tendency to want to skip "the poles" and hastily assemble their Gospel understanding. This is shortsighted because there is a set of doctrinal truths (think "poles") that is necessary for understanding the redeeming work of Christ. These glorious truths define and give shape to the essence, means, and goal of the Gospel. Yet too often, in our earnest and heartfelt desire for children to come to salvation as soon as possible, these truths are skipped, minimized, or poorly explained. Over time, this may produce confusion, doubt, and even more dangerous consequences in lives of children. Yes, there is a time and place for a very simple, summarized Gospel presentation. But we must also consider a more formal, long-term, strategic plan for teaching children the breadth and depth of the Gospel.

How can we, from the very beginning, begin to teach our children and students the glorious truths that define and shape the Gospel? What core truths must be included?[1] I would like to suggest a general strategy, one that encompasses doctrinal truths in nine key areas. In my experience in teaching the Bible to children, I have found that these are areas where we tend to be most deficient in our depth and clarity. It is also important to note that in most cases, one isolated lesson, curricula, or resource will not include truths in all nine areas. That is to be expected. Our aim should be to build a strong Gospel foundation for our children. Therefore, teaching children a series on the doctrine of God as revealed in the Old Testament is not "Gospel-less" if it is serving this long-term aim. Over the course of our children's biblical education, in which we strive to teach them the whole counsel of God, emphasizing these truths will serve to continually ground them in the glories of the Gospel.

Following are the nine areas, briefly highlighting doctrinal truths that are necessary for defining the Gospel.

1. SCRIPTURE

If we want our children to have a solid faith in Christ, one of the first questions we should address is "What is the Bible?" In many children's resources it has become common to answer this question by stating that the Bible is, first and foremost, *a story.* Stories are an excellent way to communicate with children. And yes, in one sense the Bible is a story—a true story that tells the most important message of all!

---

[1] For a child-friendly exploration of these truths, see *Helping Children to Understand the Gospel* and *Glorious God, Glorious Gospel: An Interactive Family Devotional Guide,* available from Truth78.org.

However, this characterization of Scripture fails to address the variety of literary types found in Scripture and does not convey the full weight and authority of Scripture—the "God-breathed" authority. For example, we need to teach them that,

- All the words of the Bible are God's own words. They are completely true and without error. Therefore, the Bible is the highest and final authority.
- The main message of the Bible is clear and understandable.
- The Bible is absolutely necessary for knowing, loving, trusting, and obeying God.
- The Bible makes known everything needed for salvation and the Christian life—nothing is missing.

This fuller understanding of the Bible is necessary for rightly responding to it. For example, when children read that they must "be holy, for I am holy" (1 Peter 1:15), it is not optional. It carries final authority over their lives. God is speaking, and they must listen and rightly respond. The Gospel is grounded in the Bible's authoritative, absolute, objective, unchanging, and universal truth. It is truth (John 17:17). It impacts every area of life. It calls for all of our thoughts, feelings, words, and actions to submit to its authority. Furthermore, this understanding of Scripture provides our children with a strong defense in guarding against error, false religions, and dangerous philosophies and worldviews. It provides an unshakable foundation for all of life.

2. THE TRIUNE GOD

John Piper says, "...today I think the biggest challenge [for the church] is: Do people know God...Are they getting the whole counsel of God so that they can love the whole God?"[2]

That's a strange description: "the whole God." Yet it's an apt way to put it. False doctrine arises out of a deficient or skewed view of God. And

---

[2] John Piper, *Ask Pastor John* podcast , "What Are the Biggest Challenges Facing the Evangelical Church in 2016?" https://www.desiringgod.org/interviews/what-are-the-biggest-challenges-facing-the-evangelical-church-in-2016.

sadly, even in many Bible-believing churches, a child's exposure to the "whole God" is often limited. Some believe the whole God is too much for children to handle. They're right. He *is* too much to handle. That's the point. He is God and we are not. He is beyond our finite ability to completely and fully understand whether you are 6 or 60 years old. In his classic work, *The Knowledge of the Holy*, A.W. Tozer says:

> The heaviest obligation lying upon the Christian Church today is to purify and elevate her concept of God until it is once more worthy of Him—and of her...We do the greatest service to the next generation of Christians by passing on to them undimmed and undiminished that noble concept of God which we received from our Hebrew and Christian fathers of generations past.[3]

Who will our children be more likely to grow up and be in awe of—the God of the Bible or a famous sports star or entertainment personality? It depends in part on how much we have exposed them to the awesome character of God revealed from Genesis to Revelation. Ask yourself: How many attributes of God have your students and children been taught? How deeply have they plumbed the depths of these? Here is a sampling,

ALMIGHTY, ETERNAL,
FAITHFUL, GOOD, MERCIFUL,
JEALOUS, OMNISCIENT, OMNIPRESENT,
WISE, LOVING, UNCHANGING,
RIGHTEOUS, HOLY,
INVISIBLE,SOVEREIGN,
SELF-SUFFICIENT, JUST,
WRATHFUL, PATIENT, BLESSED,
INCOMPREHENSIBLE, GLORIOUS

If we were to carefully reflect on all of God's attributes, we would see that each is reflected in the message of the Gospel. That is because

---

[3] A. W. Tozer, *The Knowledge of the Holy* (New York, NY: Harper Collins, 1961), 4.

the "whole God" is central to the Gospel message. Consider this one example from Jerry Bridges,

> The *love* of God has no meaning apart from Calvary. And Calvary has no meaning apart from the *holy* and *just wrath* of God. Jesus did not die just to give us peace and a purpose in life; He died to save us from the *wrath* of God...[4]

The Old Testament provides our children with an essential introduction to the fullness of God's character. If we simply treat the Old Testament as a quick jumping point to the cross, we risk undermining the profound meaning of salvation.

Additionally, we must be careful to help our children understand God in terms of His triune nature. There is a trend that teaches children to see and interpret that every text of the Bible points to Jesus and is about Jesus. Yes, in a manner of speaking this is completely true (see Colossians 1:15-20). But we should also consider these words by the great Presbyterian theologian J. Gresham Machen,

> ...when men say that we know God only as He is revealed in Jesus, they are denying all real knowledge of God whatever. For unless there be some idea of God independent of Jesus, the ascription of deity to Jesus has no meaning. To say, "Jesus is God," is meaningless unless the word "God" has an antecedent meaning attached to it....[5]

To understand who Jesus is, children must understand who God is. God exists eternally as the Trinity. Although this truth is mysterious and beyond full human comprehension, it is *central* to Christianity. Its proper understanding divides true Christian faith from Christian-like cults and other religions. We need to communicate the Gospel within the context of the triune nature of God. This doesn't need to be overly complex—especially at the younger

---

[4] Jerry Bridges, *The Practice of Godliness* (Colorado Springs, CO: NavPress Publishing Group, 1996), 24.
[5] J. Gresham Machen, *Christianity and Liberalism* (Grand Rapids, MI: William B. Eerdmans Publishing Company, 2009), 48-49.

ages. Children can be taught these basic statements, which can be explained further as they mature:

- There is only one God.
- God the Father is God. Jesus the Son is God. The Holy Spirit is God.
- There are three Persons in one God.

In order for our children to rightly understand the New Testament, salvation, and living the Christian life, we must emphasize the Trinity as they encounter language specifically relating to Father, Son, and Holy Spirit. They must recognize these three distinct Persons as truly and fully God—the one God—all working together in perfect unity in the work of salvation. For example, in Ephesians 1, we see the Father choosing (v. 4), the Son accomplishing (v. 7), and the Spirit guaranteeing (v. 14). Therefore, we must take great care to repeatedly remind our children of the Trinitarian nature of the Gospel.

3. MAN—WHO WE ARE IN RELATION TO GOD AND OUR PURPOSE

Once our children have a proper and basic understanding of God and the authority of His Word, they have categories and boundaries to see who man is in relation to God. For example, most church-going children know the opening sentence of the Bible,

In the beginning, God created the heavens and the earth (Genesis 1:1).

This seemingly simple verse carries profound implications. Genesis 1:1 tells us there is a God who exists. He Himself is eternal and needs nothing outside of Himself. He is independent. Everything came into being through His almighty will. Therefore, He rightly owns and governs everything. He sets the parameters for everything else—declaring what is true and right. He has authority over all.

From the very beginning, man's relationship with God is outlined and defined. We are not autonomous or independent. We are His creatures, dependent on Him for "life and breath and everything else" (Acts 17:25). We exist for God, God does not exist for us. He is our Ruler (1 Chronicles 29:12). We are accountable to Him (Hebrews 4:13). This has huge Gospel implications. For example, when our children read Jesus' words, "repent and believe in the gospel" (Mark 1:15), He is speaking as their eternal, sovereign, Creator, and Ruler. And He will hold them accountable for their response.

Once children know who they are in relation to God, we can ask the next question: Why did He create us? What is our purpose? Here are a few answers from Scripture,

...obey the voice of the LORD your God (Deuteronomy 27:10).

Delight yourself in the LORD...(Psalm 37:4)

Trust in the LORD with all your heart...(Proverbs 3:5)

Worship the LORD...(Psalm 96:9)

...love the Lord your God with all your heart and with all your soul and with all your mind (Matthew 22:37).

I give thanks to you, O Lord my God...and I will glorify your name forever (Psalm 86:12).

Scripture reveals our ultimate purpose: To glorify God as His image bearers by trusting, loving, obeying, and enjoying Him— always giving God the thanks, honor, and worship He deserves. As we communicate the Gospel to children, our relation to God and our God-given purpose should permeate our conversations. Every day the world tries to woo us and our children away from this call, promising greater joy and happiness outside of our intended purpose. Only the Bible rightly defines this relationship, and only the Gospel can bring this relationship into joyful completion.

4. THE LAW OF GOD

God is holy, and He commands His people to be holy. This holiness is so crucial that the Bible says without it, "no one will see the Lord" (Hebrews 12:14). Image bearers are to rightly reflect the holiness of their Creator (1 Peter 1:15).

We must teach children that that holy reflection is not some subjective vague feeling in our hearts. God has revealed His holiness—and the measure of our holiness—through His holy, righteous, and good commands (Romans 7:12).

Unfortunately, when some hear the words *law* or *commands,* the words *legalism* and *moralism* come to mind. Yes, we should be on guard against these prideful and deadly traps as we teach our children. R.C. Sproul helpfully summarizes the law:

> The law reflects the will of the Lawgiver, and in that regard it is intensely personal. The law reflects to the creature the perfect will of the Creator and at the same time reveals the character of that Being whose law it is.

> ...by revealing God's character, [the law] exposes our fallenness. It is the mirror that reflects our own images—warts and all—and becomes the pedagogue, the schoolmaster that drives us to Christ.[6]

The law seen in this manner, points our children to see their desperate need for a perfect, law-keeping Savior. Furthermore, God's law reflects what it then means to live as God's covenant people. "It sounds very spiritual to say God is interested in a relationship, not in rules," says Kevin DeYoung. "But it's not biblical. From top to bottom the Bible is full of commands. They aren't meant to stifle a relationship with God, but to protect it, seal it, and define it."[7] We must help our children understand why the psalmist gladly said, "Oh how I love your law!" (Psalm 119:97).

---

[6] R. C. Sproul, "Getting the Gospel Right: Interview" https://www.ligonier.org/blog/getting-gospel-right-interview-rcsproul/

[7] Kevin DeYoung, *The Hole in Our Holiness* (Wheaton, IL: Crossway, 2012), 45.

5. OUR SIN AND GOD'S JUDGMENT

If you truly understand who God is and what He is like, who you are in relation to God, and the character and function of His law, then your sin and God's judgment take on a whole new meaning—a proper Gospel meaning.

D. A. Carson says,

> There can be no agreement as to what salvation is unless there is agreement as to that from which salvation rescues us. The problem and the solution hang together...It is impossible to gain a deep grasp of what the cross achieves without plunging into a deep grasp of what sin is...
>
> ...In short, if we do not comprehend the massive role that sin plays in the Bible and therefore in biblically faithful Christianity, we shall misread the Bible.[8]

Too often—and understandably so—we want to protect our children from the ugly reality of sin. But as Carson says, our children cannot truly understand the cross apart from the essence and problem of sin. Consider for a moment a typical, brief summary of the Gospel for children,

> You are a sinner and have disobeyed God. God loves you and sent Jesus to die for your sin. If you trust in Jesus, your sin will be forgiven and you will receive eternal life.

Every word is Gospel truth. And, stated this way, many children will—at least outwardly—readily affirm it. But if this is the main or only way we talk about sin and the essence of Christ's redeeming work, have we adequately *plunged into a deep grasp of what sin is?* Consider a few texts,

> as it is written: "None is righteous, no, not one; no one understands no one seeks for God. All have turned aside; together they have become worthless; no one does good, not even one" (Romans 3:10-12).

---

[8] D. A. Carson, "Sin's Contemporary Significance," *Fallen: A Theology of Sin.* Christopher W. Morgan and Robert A. Peterson, eds. (Wheaton, IL: Crossway, 2013), 22-23.

...the wrath of God comes upon the sons of disobedience
(Ephesians 5:6b).

They will suffer the punishment of eternal destruction, away
from the presence of the Lord...(2 Thessalonians 1:9).

Based on verses like these, and many others, here is a more comprehensive view that can be communicated to children,

- You have rebelled against God's rightful authority and rule.
- You have not honored and treasured God as you should.
- Your sinful desires, thoughts, words, and actions are an offense to the holiness of God.
- Because God is holy, He can neither look upon nor ignore your sin.
- God is filled with wrath—fierce anger—toward sin.
- You deserve God's punishment of death and hell—experiencing His wrath forever.
- You are completely and utterly helpless to save yourself.

This more expanded explanation may seem harsh and even shocking to a child. It may prove to make them upset and sad. But at some point, early in their lives, we need to show them their true condition before a holy God. By giving them time to ponder the grievousness of their sin and God's just condemnation, it serves as a pathway to the glory of Christ.

6. THE PERSON AND WORK OF CHRIST

Most children from Christian homes and our churches are well acquainted with the wonderful Gospel narratives about Jesus. They learn that He is the long-promised Savior, the Son of God. They learn of His miracles—proving that He is fully God while being fully man. His parables, teaching, and life all serve to reveal the glory of God. These are all basic truths we need to communicate to our children.

What is often less clear to them is *why* Jesus died and *what* His death and resurrection accomplished. This is why they need a robust understanding of *justification*. Salvation (and therefore the Gospel) hangs on the meaning of justification. While saying, "Jesus died on the cross to save you from your sins" has a place especially for younger children, as they mature we must expand upon this. Jesus' death involves a legal act whereby God forgives sin, gives His people Jesus' righteousness, and declares His sinful people righteous. This may sound academic at first glance but if children have been given the proper "antecedents" (God is holy, just, wrathful, merciful, loving, etc.), explaining justification will not involve wholly new concepts.

Using truths previously learned, you can provide children with a deep, rich account of what happened on the cross—the justification of sinners—by explaining a few select verses. Here is an example of how this could be done,

> He himself bore our sins in his body on the tree, that we might die to sin and live to righteousness...(1 Peter 2:24a)

> He is the propitiation for our sins, (1 John 2:2a)

> Because Jesus always obeyed God and was sinless (righteous), He was able to be the perfect substitute for sinners. How? While Jesus hung on the cross, God took the sins of all the people whom He specially loved and placed them on Jesus. (Think of taking a bunch of icky garbage and placing it in a clean plastic bag.)

> So there was Jesus, now carrying many, many sins. What does God feel toward sin? Wrath. (Remember that wrath is fierce anger) [Romans 1:18]. What is the right punishment? Death [Romans 6:23a]. So even though no one could see it with their eyes, while Jesus hung on the cross, God poured out all His fierce anger at sin on Jesus. God punished His own Son to death.

> ...Jesus received God's punishment willingly so that His people would never, ever, ever have to receive it. That way, God's people would receive God's smile, instead of His wrathful frown. That's what the word propitiation means. Jesus received God's wrath so that we could receive His smile.

...[But when Jesus] died on the cross, He didn't just take away some-thing from His people (their sin). He also gave them something. What is it? His perfect righteousness (perfect obedience). Now God's people would be able to live with God forever![9]

Jesus' resurrection is proof that He did this!

7. SALVATION AS THE FREE GIFT OF GOD FOR ALL WHO REPENT AND BELIEVE

Here is a beautiful text that every child should memorize,

For by grace you have been saved through faith. And this is not your own doing; it is the gift of God, not a result of works, so that no one may boast. For we are his workmanship, created in Christ Jesus for good works, which God prepared beforehand, that we should walk in them (Ephesians 2:8-10).

As the solas of the Reformation summarize: Salvation is by grace alone, through faith alone, in Christ alone. But there is a caution here that we must consider, especially when teaching children. We need to carefully define and explain these terms for our children.

"By grace." Grace is unmerited favor. God is giving us something we do not deserve nor could we ever earn. It means God gives salva-tion to whoever He pleases. It means understanding our emptiness and worthlessness before God. Do our children understand this in sufficient measure? Or are they coming to Christ with any sense of entitlement or pride?

Free "gift." Children love gifts. Who wouldn't want to receive the best gift of all—salvation! But consider this statement by John MacArthur, "salvation is the free gift that will cost you everything." This is the cost expressed when Jesus said, "If anyone would come after me, let him deny himself and take up his cross daily and follow me." (Luke 9:23) Do our children have an age-appropriate grasp of this? What, at minimum, might trusting in Christ cost them? Are

---

[9] Jill Nelson, *God's Gospel* (Phillipsburg, NJ: P&R Publishing, 2015), 103-104.

you encouraging them to count the cost as you earnestly encourage them to trust Christ?

"Faith" includes a right understanding of certain facts about who Jesus is and what He has done, and a complete dependence on Him for all that He is doing, has done, and will do. Many children readily affirm true facts about Jesus, but coming to wholly depend on Him as Lord and Savior for all of life involves a much deeper, personal commitment. Additionally, we must impress on them that true saving faith is always accompanied by repentance—a deep-felt sorrow and hatred of sin, such that you turn to Jesus and commit to follow Him always (Mark 1:15, 2 Corinthians 7:10).

Along with emphasizing what Christ saves us *from*, we need to also explain what Christ saves us *for*. True saving faith will be evidenced by good works. We must carefully define these good works in terms of active, daily, grace-dependent, Spirit-empowered submission to Jesus and His ways. Again, there is an age appropriateness that needs to be considered here, but we need to impress the necessity of growth in godliness in the Christian life.

As parents and teachers, we need to be careful, discerning, and patient. We often mistake spiritual curiosity for true, saving faith. We mistakenly think that because a child expresses a "love" for Jesus it means that he or she is saved. Even a child's tears when acknowledging sin against God don't necessarily mean a child has truly repented.[10]

Our great hope is this: God is sovereign over every child's salvation. Repeatedly teach the truths of the Gospel, lovingly implore them to trust Christ, and pray that the Holy Spirit would bring about new spiritual life.

8. THE CHURCH AND GOD'S KINGDOM— LIVING WITHIN GOD'S REDEEMED FAMILY, UNDER GOD'S RULE

The Gospel is very personal, calling each of us to believe on Jesus and be saved. But Jesus died and rose again in order to create a special

---

[10] For more helpful guidance concerning a child's profession of faith, I highly recommend *The Faith of a Child* (Moody Press, 2000) by Art Murphy and *Your Child's Profession of Faith* (Grace and Truth Books, 2010) by Dennis Gundersen.

family of God—the church. Our children must be introduced to this greater family. While the church does include every single Christian from all over the world, God has also given us local churches. The gathered church is to focus on three main goals: worship of God, equipping and encouraging the saints for a life of godliness, and proclaiming the Gospel to the lost.

Even before our children come to saving faith, we must communicate to them the importance of the church and what family life includes. Here are a few examples,

- Make regular attendance at the weekly service a high priority and explain the elements of the service.
- Teach children about the roles of pastors, elders, and teachers.
- Identify and model the "one another" commands.
- Involve them in serving within the church and its ministries.
- Participate in evangelism and world missions.

It is tragic the number of Christians who don't believe in the importance of committing to a local church and being actively involved in its life and ministries. We can help prevent this by connecting the Gospel to the building of Jesus' church.

9. THE GOAL OF THE GOSPEL IS ENJOYING GOD FOREVER

Imagine asking your children or students the following question: What do you think is the best thing about living forever in heaven? I must admit that my answer, even as a young adult, would have missed the mark of what is truly the greatest joy of eternal life. I mistakenly believed that the end goal of the Gospel was enjoying eternal life in heaven, with all the benefits of a glorified body, no more sin and suffering, perfect peace, etc.

When I came upon these words by John Piper everything changed:

...the highest, best, final, decisive good of the gospel, without which no other gifts would be good, is the glory of God in the face of Christ revealed for our everlasting enjoyment. The saving love of God is God's commitment to do everything necessary to enthrall us with what is most deeply and durably satisfying, namely himself.[11]

This Godward goal is expressed throughout Scripture. One example is Psalm 16:11,

You make known to me the path of life; in your presence there is fullness of joy; at your right hand our pleasures forevermore.

The "path of life" is the Gospel. From beginning to end, the Gospel is about God. He is the source, means, and goal of the Gospel. Our children need to be taught this with persistent intentionality. They were created to be awed and fully satisfied by one thing alone—God.

While we must acknowledge that we are not decisive in their salvation, we are called to do everything in our power to enthrall children with God. We are called to present them with the amazing and all-satisfying truth of the glory of God in the face of Christ. We have the great privilege and grave responsibility to share with them the only means of obtaining this everlasting enjoyment—the Gospel!

JILL NELSON is the co-author of the Truth78 curriculum, devotionals, and books. She and her husband, Bruce, have two grown children and five grandchildren.

---

[11] John Piper, *God Is the Gospel* (Wheaton, IL: Crossway Books, 2005), 13.

8

Sovereign Grace and the Salvation of Children

There is no such thing as a seeker

C.J. MAHANEY

IF I UNDERSTAND our Savior correctly, He would define true greatness as serving others for the glory of God. This is greatness in the eyes of God—greatness that is derived as a substitutionary sacrifice for our sins, and not the fruit of some moral superiority resident within us. This is the biblical definition of greatness. And this is what those of you who teach the Bible to children do. You serve for the benefit of others.

If you are involved in teaching the Bible and proclaiming the Gospel to children in your church, I pray you will be richly rewarded as you observe the fruit of your labors. But your richest reward awaits that final day, when the Savior Himself will say, "Well done." Your labor is not in vain. I pray none of you will grow weary. What teachers and parents and pastors are doing is of vital importance to the plan and purpose of God.

I hope that in what follows, you might be *personally* refreshed by the grace of God. Let us listen carefully as we are addressed by God Himself,

> Blessed be the God and Father of our Lord Jesus Christ, who has blessed us in Christ with every spiritual blessing in the heavenly places, even as he chose us in him before the foundation of the world, that we should be holy and blameless before him...(Ephesians 1:3-4).

Have you ever thought about how reflecting on your own story of conversion, and the roots in eternity past, can serve your soul? James Cantelon's recollection of his conversion experience is as moving as it is insightful:

> "First impressions are lasting impressions." So goes the old saying, and I suspect in most cases it is true. My first impression of God is with me to this day. It happened at a musty old church camp in central Saskatchewan, Canada. I was five years old.
>
> Back in those days we were into tabernacles. Not only were most of our churches called tabernacles, but our camp meeting buildings were also given this Old Testament name for tent. On one especially hot day my parents were in the adult tabernacle, and I, with my fellow junior campers, was in the children's tabernacle. The teacher was taking us through Bunyan's *Pilgrim's Progress*. As she taught, something sparked within me.
>
> After the lesson the children exploded into the sunshine to play. I lingered. Miss Brown seemed to know why.
>
> "Can I help you, Jimmy?" she asked gently. I nodded dumbly, biting my suddenly trembling lower lip, tears welling in my eyes.
>
> "Let's go into the back room and pray," she said. I can't explain what happened...But I will say this: at age five I suddenly felt as though

I were the worst sinner who had ever lived. My sense of sin nearly crushed my little heart. The prayer, however, had not ended. It began with remorse, it grew into joy. I felt this newly discovered burden lift from my fragile soul. The presence of God overwhelmed me. Without my looking for him, or asking for him—indeed, without any knowledge of my need of him—God came looking for me, asking for me...a five-year-old kid.[1]

First impressions are lasting impressions. I find Mr. Cantelon's description of his conversion experience revealing: "God came looking for me." How would you describe your conversion experience? Do you perceive, like Mr. Cantelon, that God came looking for you? Or is your first impression of your conversion experience, primarily, your pursuit of God? As you reflect upon your conversion experience, is the accent on the initiative and intervention of God, or on your response of repentance and faith?

Because first impressions are lasting impressions, we must examine those impressions in light of the objective truth of Scripture to determine whether our first impressions of our conversion are indeed biblical and, therefore, accurate.

There are detrimental effects to having an inaccurate first impression of our conversion. There are serious consequences when we misunderstand or misinterpret our conversion experience. Here's the good news: There are wonderful life-changing, life-transforming benefits when we rightly understand our conversion experience.

Ephesians 1:4 addresses first impressions. We must submit all first impressions to this text for it reveals what really happened at the moment of conversion. And even more remarkably, this text reveals what preceded the moment of conversion. This passage informs us that our transition from death to life, from sinner to saint, from object of wrath to object of mercy, was exclusively and entirely the result of sovereign grace. Regardless of your first impression of your conversion experience, what we find in Ephesians 1:4 is the biblical explanation of your conversion experience: "...he chose us in him

---

[1] James Cantelon, *Theology for Non-Theologians* (New York, NY: Macmillan, 1988), 3.

before the foundation of the world that we should be holy and blameless before him."

In this text, Paul turns our attention away from our personal experience and our first impressions of it, and he directs our attention to God, to eternity past, to divine election, to sovereign grace.

We are swimming in the deep end of the theological pool with this topic. The mere introduction of it raises certain questions. The most frequent question I receive when I teach on sovereign grace or divine election is, "How do we reconcile divine sovereignty and human responsibility?"

Well, the smartest minds in church history have been unable to do so! Sovereignty involves an element of mystery. Get comfortable with mystery because you will always be bumping into mystery in relationship to God—not only in this life, but in the life to come! We shouldn't be surprised when we encounter mystery. Mystery is inevitable when our subject is God. In fact, God has announced that we can expect mystery: "The secret things belong to the LORD our God, but the things that are revealed belong to us and to our children forever..." (Deuteronomy 29:29). God's eye is always on the children, the next generation.

Now, I have to submit to you, in my arrogance, mystery is not my preference. I don't mind people having secrets, but I want to be in the know! Pastoring in Washington D.C. for 27 years, we had numerous people in our church who did secret stuff for the government. They knew stuff that I wanted to know! It wasn't hard to spot them because their answers to my questions were vague and general, "I work for the government..." To which I'd reply, "Sure. What department? FBI, CIA, NSA, which one?" I tried not to provoke them because I understand there are commitments they make, and I want to honor that. But they can trust me! At times, in my arrogance, that's how I relate to God.

My curiosity about that which is secret, I'm convinced, is normally motivated by pride. I must recognize this temptation and resist this tendency, particularly in relation to the doctrine of election. This is a temptation and tendency particularly present when you teach on election.

Let's consider the very wise counsel of John Calvin:

> The subject of predestination, which in itself is attended by considerable difficulty, is rendered very perplexed, and hence perilous, by human curiosity, which cannot be restrained from wandering into forbidden paths...Those secrets of his will which he has seen fit to manifest, are revealed in his Word—revealed in so far as he knew to be conducive to our interest and welfare...Let it, therefore, be our first principle that to desire any other knowledge of predestination than that which is expounded by the Word of God, is no less infatuated than to walk where there is no path, or to seek light in darkness...The best rule of sobriety is, not only in learning to follow wherever God leads, but also when he makes an end of teaching to cease wishing to be wise.[2]

I understand human curiosity. You might want to wander into a forbidden path. You might be distracted by an arrogant desire for a secret. Let us restrain this curiosity and let us recognize that God has, in His wisdom, commanded us not to seek knowledge where He has not revealed it in His Word. This is for our good.

How comfortable are you with mystery? With paradox? With apparent contradiction? As I understand it, maturity involves an increasing comfort with mystery and a growing trust in God, so that we can say with David, "my heart is not lifted up...I do not occupy myself with things too great and too marvelous for me" (Psalm 131:1). As the years pass, as you mature in the Christian life, there won't be less mystery. But hopefully there will be more humility, making us more at rest with mystery.

I cannot reconcile divine sovereignty and human responsibility for you. It's a secret. It hasn't been revealed. There is an element of mystery involved with the doctrine of election. Calvin said it well; the subject in itself "is attended by considerable difficulty." And so we must address and teach the topic both humbly and wisely. If the

---

[2] John Calvin, *Institutes of the Christian Religion* (Peabody, MA: Hendrickson Publishers, Inc., 2008), 607-609.

doctrine of election is mishandled or misunderstood, it can have a detrimental effect rather than its intended beneficial effect.

Before we look at the doctrine of election, I have some qualifying statements that I hope will prevent misunderstanding and will prepare your hearts for our study and journey together.

1. THE DOCTRINE OF ELECTION, though very important, does not define us. The Gospel defines us. I am passionate about election, but I am not more passionate about election than I am about the Gospel. The Gospel is of first importance. The doctrine of election plays a critical protective role in relation to the Gospel. It protects and preserves the Gospel of grace, but election is not the Gospel. The Gospel is the person and work of Jesus Christ in His substitutionary sacrifice on the cross. The core of the Gospel is summed up by Paul when he writes "For I delivered to you as of first importance what I also received: that Christ died for our sins in accordance with the Scriptures, that he was buried, that he was raised on the third day in accordance with the Scriptures" (1 Corinthians 15:3-4). Trusting in Him and His finished work is what saves us.

2. A PERSON DOES NOT have to believe in the doctrine of election to be saved. A saving relationship with God does not require an understanding of, or an agreement with the doctrine of election. A saving relationship with God requires repentance from sin and trust in Christ alone, to save by grace alone, through faith alone.

3. OUR UNITY WITH other Christians does not require full agreement on the doctrine of election. Charles Spurgeon wrote the following:

> We give our hand to every man that loves the Lord Jesus Christ, be he what he may or who he may. The doctrine of election, like the great act of election itself, is intended to divide, not between Israel and Israel, but between Israel and the Egyptians. Not between saint and saint, but between saints and the children of the world. A man

may be evidently of God's chosen family and yet, though elected, may not believe in the doctrine of election. I hold that there are many savingly called who do not believe in effectual calling and that there are a great many who persevere to the end who do not believe the doctrine of final perseverance. We do hope the hearts of many are a great deal better than their heads. We do not set their fallacies down to any willful opposition to the truth as it is in Jesus, but simply to an error in their judgment which we pray God to correct. We hope that if they think us mistaken, too, they will reciprocate the same Christian courtesy. And when we meet around the cross, we hope that we shall ever feel that we are one in Christ Jesus.[3]

4. THE DOCTRINE OF ELECTION is for Christians, not for non-Christians. This is not the message we proclaim to non-Christians. This is the message we proclaim to Christians.

Now that we've acknowledged the mystery and difficulty related to the doctrine of election, let's devote our attention to the clarity and certainty that is revealed in Scripture about sovereign grace. Yes, there is mystery in God in relation to election, but there is also clarity and certainty.

God has asserted in Scripture both divine sovereignty and human responsibility. He hasn't sought to reconcile them for us. It appears that for Him they are harmonized and that should be sufficient for us. We find both in Scripture. Therefore, we should teach both. We should teach whatever we encounter in a text. Sometimes we encounter both in the same text! But while we teach both, unarguably, the accent in Scripture is clearly on the sovereignty of God, and on the sovereignty of God in salvation.

Anthony Hoekema has wisely written,

We must therefore affirm both God's sovereignty and man's responsibility; both God's sovereign grace and our active participation in the process of salvation. We can only do justice to biblical teaching

---

[3] Charles Haddon Spurgeon, Sermon no. 324. "Effects of Sound Doctrine." *New Park Street Pulpit,* vol. 6. https://www.spurgeon.org/resource-library/sermons/effects-of-sound-doctrine#flipbook/

if we firmly hold on to both sides of the paradox. But since God is the Creator and we are his creatures, God must have the priority. Hence we must maintain that the ultimately decisive factor in the process of our salvation is the sovereign grace of God.[4]

The decisive factor in determining who is to be saved from sin is not the decision of the human beings concerned, but the sovereign grace of God. I'm not minimizing the role of repentance and faith. I'm not minimizing the role of human decision. They play a significant role in the process but they are not the ultimately decisive factor.

In Ephesians 1:4, the sovereignty of God has the priority. Here, in this passage, inspired by the spirit of God, Paul makes it very clear that the decisive factor in our conversion is the sovereign grace of God.

Let's consider and be freshly affected by sovereign grace together. If necessary, reevaluate your first impression of your conversion and submit that impression to the authoritative, accurate assertions about the ultimately decisive factor in our salvation. Let us be submissive to divine clarity and certainty as revealed in this passage and, I would argue, throughout holy Scripture.

We begin with a definition of election. J. I. Packer has written,

The verb elect means "to select, or choose out." The biblical doctrine of election is that before creation, God selected out of the human race, foreseen as fallen, those whom he would redeem, bring to faith, justify, and glorify in and through Jesus Christ...This divine choice is an expression of free and sovereign grace, for it is unconstrained and unconditional, not merited by anything in those who are its subjects. God owes sinners no mercy of any kind, only condemnation; so it is a wonder, and matter for endless praise, that he should choose to save any of us; and doubly so when his choice involved the giving of his own Son to suffer as sin-bearer for the elect.[5]

---

4 Anthony Hoekema, *Saved by Grace* (Grand Rapids, MI: Eerdmans, 1989), 3, 7.
5 J. I. Packer, *God's Words* (Downers Grove, IL: InterVarsity, 1981), 158.

With the help of this definition, let us consider Ephesians 1:4, "...he chose us in him before the foundation of the world that we should be holy and blameless before him."

It is here that we discover the following: If you have turned from your sins and trusted in the person and work of Christ, you were chosen in Christ, chosen before time, and chosen to be holy and blameless.

CHOSEN IN CHRIST

Look carefully at these three words: "He chose us." Notice where Paul begins his celebration of spiritual blessing. "He chose us." Divine choice precedes human response, and it must, in light of our sinfulness, pervasive depravity, and wicked hostility toward God. Apart from divine choice, there would be no human response. If He didn't choose me, I would never choose Him.

If we don't understand this point in particular, we will be vulnerable to misunderstanding divine election. Author Mark Webb helps prevent our misunderstanding,

> After giving a brief survey of these doctrines of sovereign grace, I asked for questions from the class. One lady, in particular, was quite troubled. She said, "This is the most awful thing I've ever heard! You make it sound as if God is intentionally turning away men who would be saved, receiving only the elect." I answered her in this vein. "You misunderstand the situation. You're visualizing...God...standing at the door of heaven, and men are thronging to get in the door, and God is saying to various ones, 'Yes, you may come, but not you, or you, or you...' The situation is hardly this. Rather, God stands at the door of heaven with his arms outstretched, inviting all to come. Yet all men without exception are running in the opposite direction toward hell as hard as they can go. So God, in election, graciously reaches out and stops this one, and that one, and this one over here, and that one over there, and effectually draws them to himself by changing their hearts, making them willing to come. Election keeps no one out of heaven who would otherwise have been there, but it keeps a whole multitude of sinners out of hell who otherwise would have been there. Were it not for election, heaven would be an empty place, and hell would be bursting at the seams."

That kind of response, grounded as I believe that it is in scriptural truth, does put a different complexion on things, doesn't it? If you perish in hell, blame yourself, as it is entirely your fault. But if you should make it to heaven, credit God, for that is entirely his work! To him alone belong all praise and glory, for salvation is all of grace from start to finish![6]

That is the situation. All people, without exception, running toward hell as hard as they can go. That was me prior to conversion. I was passionately running a race toward hell.

In the mystery of His mercy and through the preaching of the Gospel, God called me and rescued me. Paul informs me here that the call I experienced in time, through the preaching of the Gospel, originated in eternity past. God chose me. God's choice preceded yours and mine, and apart from His gracious choice, we never would have chosen Him. Are you aware of that? Are you aware that long before you chose Him, He chose you? The more you are aware of divine initiative and personal depravity, the more you will be amazed by the grace of God. You didn't discover God. He revealed Himself to you. Be careful when sharing your conversion experience and using the language of discovery when you refer to your conversion experience, regardless of your first impressions.

It's become quite popular in the church growth movement to identify a non-Christian as a *seeker*. It's a very flattering, non-offensive description, but it's neither accurate nor is it harmless. It is in fact a misrepresentation of God and a misrepresentation of us. In Scripture God is revealed as the seeker, not sinners. Sinners are revealed as those who are running as hard as they can towards hell.

I'm not denying that there are those who seek, but what they seek for is a god made in their image, not the God revealed in the Bible. It doesn't serve to identify them as seekers. No wonder there are so many Christians who are not amazed by the grace of God. They are convinced, "I found Him." As if He were hiding, or difficult to reach. They finally wore Him out, tracked Him down, and with reluctance,

[6] Mark Webb, "What Difference Does it Make?" *Reformation and Revival Journal,* vol. 3, no. 1, Winter 1994, 53-54.

He forgave them. Well, if that's your impression, no wonder you're not amazed by grace! No wonder you're not secure in grace!

Why am I a Christian? Why are you a Christian? Here's why: because God graciously and amazingly chose you. That's why. Listen again to Charles Spurgeon,

> I believe the doctrine of election, because I am quite certain that, if God had not chosen me, I should never have chosen him; and I am sure he chose me before I was born, or else he never would have chosen me afterwards; and he must have elected me for reasons unknown to me, for I never could find any reason in myself why he should have looked upon me with special love.[7]

That's the biblical explanation for each and every conversion: God chose us. He chose us in Him. Chosen *in Him.*

For God to choose us, sin must be overcome. His righteous wrath must be satisfied. The divine dilemma of His holy hostility toward sinners and our wicked hostility toward God must be resolved. Paul's letter to the Ephesians could not be more clear that Jesus is the answer to the problem of sin. If you read the first 14 verses of Ephesians 1, Jesus Christ is referenced 15 times.

Here is the means by which God's choice to save is achieved: sovereign grace is in Him—in Jesus Christ. Christians are chosen solely in Christ and solely because of Christ. Not apart from Christ, and not because of anything within us. No, sovereign grace is in Him. Election, redemption, adoption, forgiveness of sin, is in Him. There is no election, redemption, adoption, forgiveness of sin, apart from Him. He chose us. He chose us *in Him:* Jesus Christ, the Lamb slain, before the foundation of the world.

CHOSEN BEFORE TIME

Ephesians 1:4 takes your breath away. May we never grow overly familiar with the phrase, "before the foundation of the world." When did this choosing happen? *Before* the foundation of the world.

---

[7] Charles Spurgeon, quoted in *Table Talk,* September 8, 1994.

This is a rare biblical reference revealing what God was busy doing before time, before creation, before the foundation of the world. We know little of His activities before time, but we do know this. He was busy finalizing His plan, and this plan would involve the most unlikely choice of sinners like you and me.

He chose us before the foundation of the world. Prior to Genesis 1:1, sinners like you and me were singled out by God Himself. Worthy only of His wrath, richly deserving only the full and furious righteous wrath of God, we were instead chosen before time, by name. It takes your breath away. May God's electing grace create tears of gratefulness and hearts filled with awe and affection.

CHOSEN TO BE HOLY AND BLAMELESS

What is the practical effect of election? What difference should it make in our lives personally and in our ministries to children? This has a purpose; a divinely intended effect. It exists for our benefit.

The effect or fruit of sovereign grace is,

1. HUMILITY BEFORE GOD

The church in Corinth, which Paul addressed, was in need of humility. Their arrogance was pronounced. Paul reminds them of the doctrine of election as a means of addressing their pride. It would appear that Paul is adjusting first impressions of the Corinthian church about their conversion that were not accurate. In 1 Corinthians 1:26-29, he writes,

> For consider your calling, brothers: not many of you were wise according to worldly standards, not many were powerful, not many were of noble birth. But God chose what is foolish in the world to shame the wise; God chose what is weak in the world to shame the strong; God chose what is low and despised in the world, even things that are not, to bring to nothing things that are, so that no human being might boast in the presence of God.

Three times he reminds them that God chose them, and then he reminds them why. Mark Webb says, "God intentionally designed salvation so that no man could boast of it...He didn't merely arrange it so that boasting would be discouraged or kept to a minimum—He planned it so that boasting would be absolutely excluded. Election does precisely that."[8]

Sovereign grace leaves no room for self-congratulation. It eliminates all human achievement and every human contribution. Election is devastating to pride. What do you think was the ultimately decisive factor in your salvation? Was it your decision? Your repentance? If so, then you would have something to boast about. In light of sovereign grace, the compelling, unanswered question is not, "Why isn't my relative saved?" It is, "Why am I saved?"

There is only one biblical explanation in light of my pervasive depravity. In light of the fact that I was running as fast and as hard as I could toward hell, and encouraging others to run hard and fast with me toward hell, there is only one explanation: sovereign grace.

My testimony is a dramatic one. I grew up in a nominally Roman Catholic family. At an early age, I stopped attending mass and rebelled against all things Catholic. From an early age, I did not fear authority. I was not afraid of my parents; I was not intimidated by them. Through the influence of older friends—though I'm ultimately responsible and all of this is to my shame—I was immersed in the drug culture. I had no category for the Gospel. One evening, a friend of mine who had recently moved to Fort Lauderdale, Florida, went to a Baptist church where he heard the Gospel. He experienced the miracle of regeneration. He repented. He trusted in Christ. A few weeks later, he returned to Maryland on a mission. Because I was his friend, he came to where I lived with one purpose—to share the Gospel with me.

That evening when my friend dropped by my house, I began to smoke hash. He was immersed in the drug culture and had been a main influence in introducing me to the drug culture. When I asked him to join me, he declined. I was perplexed, but I wasn't going to be deterred. So as I began to smoke hash—it wasn't three weeks since his conversion—he shared the Gospel with me, what he understood of the Gospel and the Savior's sacrifice on the cross for my sins. I had never

---

[8] Mark Web, 52.

heard the Gospel in my life prior to that moment. I had never read a Bible, had never even opened a Bible. That evening, as he shared the Gospel, God acted upon me. I wasn't immediately reformed doctrinally. But I was reformed experientially. If you had talked to me that night and said, "Who initiated this?" I would have said, "God acted upon me. I didn't initiate this." My life was dramatically changed.

My friends and family were perplexed when they encountered me the next morning. They could not understand what happened to me. It was just inconceivable. For years, particularly after starting a church, I had individuals—not just friends, but even teachers from my high school—who didn't have a category for my conversion and could *not* believe that I was a pastor of the church. They would come on Sundays just to see if what they had heard was true. I was a mystery to them! They couldn't reconcile the C. J. they knew with the C. J. they were hearing about.

What explanation is there for my conversion? It was not my moral or intellectual superiority. The only explanation is sovereign grace! God chose me, and I experienced that choice through His effectual call and the preaching of the Gospel at a moment in time, so that there would be no doubt who was responsible, and no boasting in His presence.

Regardless of your background, your conversion was no different. You may say, "You don't understand, I was converted at four. My serious sin was 'not sharing my Legos.' That's all I've got to work with!" Well, in the mystery of His mercy, God determined that you wouldn't live a life of sin and shame like I did. But you were no less depraved. You can, if anything, be more grateful that you were protected from years of sin. His intervention in your life is no less stunning and amazing.

The more you study the doctrine of sin and relate it to when you were four, the more amazed you will be that God intervened at five. Because, if He didn't, at six and seven and nine and 10 and 15, you would have been running toward hell as hard and as fast as you could. But before you could run too far toward hell, God intervened in your life. How kind of Him! Why did He do that? For His glory and our humility.

That's why it's a contradiction for someone to teach election arrogantly. It should always be taught humbly. If election is not taught humbly, it has been misunderstood and misapplied.

2. ASSURANCE FROM GOD

The fruit of election is assurance from God. I still meet too many Christians who aren't assured in their heart that God loves them, personally. To understand election is to experience the personal love of God. Election is the after-the-experience explanation of your conversion. Revisit your moment of conversion, informed by Ephesians 1:4, and you will realize and receive God's love for you. This text reveals what happened at the moment of conversion, and most importantly, what preceded that moment of conversion.

Philip Ryken may help us here:

> The famous American Bible teacher Donald Grey Barnhouse often used an illustration to help people make sense of election. He asked them to imagine a cross like the one on which Jesus died, only so large that it had a door in it. Over the door were these words from Revelation: "Whosoever will may come." These words represent the free and universal offer of the Gospel. By God's grace, the message of salvation is for everyone. Every man, woman, and child who will come to the cross is invited to believe in Jesus Christ and enter eternal life.
>
> On the other side of the door a happy surprise awaits the one who believes and enters. From the inside, anyone glancing back can see these words from Ephesians written above the door: "Chosen in Christ before the foundation of the world." Election is best understood in hindsight, for it is only after coming to Christ that one can know whether one has been chosen in Christ. Those who make a decision for Christ find that God made a decision for them in eternity past.[9]

Happy surprise, indeed! Know, experience, and feel the love of God for you personally, informed by Ephesians 1:4. Hear God say to you, "I have loved you with an everlasting love. Begun in eternity past, it will extend to eternity future, my love for you." It's stated vividly and emotionally in Ephesians 1:5 where we are referred to as "adopted." Adopted by God. Listen to David Wells:

---

[9] Philip Ryken, *The Message of Salvation* (Downers Grove, IL: InterVarsity, 2001), 60.

That God has planned our redemption from all eternity delivers a declaration louder than any thunderclap. It is that he is for us, that he has always been for us. He was for us in the far reaches of eternity. It was there he took thoughts of us even before we existed. It was there that he planned to act for us. This plan was there from the very beginning. He planned to do this knowing that once we fell into the disorder of sin our fist would be raised against him. But his grace preceded us. It preempted our refusal to submit to him. He did for us what we could not do for ourselves. He refused to abandon us as orphans in the world. On the contrary, from all eternity he planned to effect our rescue and adoption. Can we find a more reassuring word than this?[10]

Feel God's love. That is the effect of election.

3. GRATEFULNESS TO GOD

Ephesians 1:1-14 is like one uninterrupted outburst of praise. It appears Paul doesn't even take a breath. The effect of sovereign grace is gratefulness, praise, and worship. You have this threefold phrase throughout the passage in verses 6, 12, and 14, "to the praise of His glorious grace." This doctrine of election is not meant to be an occasion for theological disputation. It is a call to worship.

4. MISSION FOR THE GLORY OF GOD

We don't preach election to the lost; we preach the Gospel. Here's the good news: Election ensures the Gospel we preach will be effective. That should free you from assuming full responsibility for the children you are teaching, and free you to trust in the One who is ultimately responsible. The doctrine of election allows believers to have faith that when they share the Gospel, God's plan and purpose cannot ultimately be frustrated, for that Gospel will be effective, because in eternity past He has chosen those He will save in and through Jesus Christ. This isn't a hindrance to evangelism. This is a motivation for evangelism, knowing that with certainty, this Gospel is assured of

---

[10] David Wells, *God in the Whirlwind* (Wheaton, IL: Crossway, 2014), 135-36.

effectiveness in the hearts of those who have been chosen in eternity past. It's not a deterrent. It's a wonderful motivation.

The next time you are teaching five-year-olds like young James Cantelon, you won't know whom God has chosen, but you can know that the Gospel is the power of God unto salvation, secured in eternity past, and assured of its effectiveness, even upon the hearts of five-year-olds. Let this increase your faith for your work in serving children. May we arise tomorrow more humble, more secure in God's love, and more grateful. God has called us and equipped us with a Gospel that is indeed the power of God, and its progress and effectiveness is assured because of what God has already determined in eternity past. This can and should have a dramatic effect on your soul that can and will be obvious to the children you serve, and this can and will have a dramatic effect on how you serve those entrusted to your care in children's ministry. All of this is to and for the praise of His glorious, sovereign grace.

C. J. MAHANEY serves as the Senior Pastor for Sovereign Grace Church of Louisville, KY. C. J. and his wife, Carolyn, have three married daughters, one son, and twelve grandchildren.

9

Showing Children
the Authority
of Jesus

*The only way to war against
the powers of darkness*

RUSSELL MOORE

IF YOU GET A PRESCRIPTION for blood pressure medication, there's going to be a warning label on it, "Keep this away from children." If you buy a set of kitchen knives, there's going to be a warning label on it, "Keep this away from children." If you go to a theme park, some of the scary rides there will have signs, "Must be this tall to ride this ride."

I never thought that I would see a warning label on the Gospel of Jesus Christ.

Then several years ago a couple of pastors in Raleigh, North Carolina, were preparing and working through their Sunday school curriculum as they were looking toward Holy Week—the week leading up to Easter. What they found was that in the curriculum that they had ordered, there was no crucifixion or resurrection of Jesus on Easter Week. They thought someone must have had an oversight.

There's some kind of a problem; they're working too far ahead that they don't understand they forgot to put the crucifixion in Holy Week. So they called up the curriculum maker, and said, "We want to tell you about this oversight." And they were told, "There is no oversight. This was intentional." The curriculum maker said, "We have concluded that this is too scary for children." They went on to say, "We understand that Easter is a very special time for churches and for Christians, but we also understand that due to the mature and graphic nature of some elements of the Easter story, the crucifixion specifically, we need to be very careful what we tell preschoolers about these things. So, we did not end the story with the crucifixion and the resurrection. We ended the story with the Last Supper in which Jesus is eating with his friends."

This was their direct quote: "We have made this choice because the crucifixion is simply too violent for preschoolers, and if we were to stop at the crucifixion and go straight to the resurrection, the preschoolers will be confused."

You think?

"Instead," they said, "our lesson this week is going to be, 'Jesus wants to be my forever friend,' however, we have provided for those churches that have asked for it, an alternate ending to the curriculum, in which you can discuss the crucifixion and the resurrection of Jesus."

An alternate ending!

What kind of a world do we live in when the *alternate* ending to the Easter story is the Easter story?! There's more going on here than one curriculum developer, than one approach to children's ministry. Behind that is an entire understanding of the way that we see what it is that we are doing when we teach and train up the next generation.

The Bible tells us that there are different stages of understanding and of life, different areas and aspects of the maturity it takes to understand some things in the natural order and some things in the Bible, and the way that we communicate them. We communicate the virgin birth to a 5-year-old very differently than we communicate it to a 55-year-old.

The question here is whether the scariness of the Gospel is foundational to children's ministry. Is Christ and Him crucified where we ultimately end up? Or, is it where we start, continue, and finish? That is what's at stake when we are preaching and teaching the Bible to children. The Apostle Paul says to the church at Ephesus that the life of the church is very similar to the life of an individual. You start off as an infant, and grow to be a child, on into "mature manhood" (Ephesians 4:13), as you are receiving the nourishment of the Word within the body. You grow up, as Paul says, into "the fullness of Christ." There is a maturing taking place.

What I want to suggest to you is that if we do not have an understanding of authority that is grounded and rooted and fueled in the Gospel, we will never reach the next generation of children with the Gospel of Jesus Christ.

Let's look together at the Gospel of Mark, chapter 1:

> Now after John was arrested, Jesus came into Galilee, proclaiming the gospel of God, and saying, "The time is fulfilled, and the kingdom of God is at hand; repent and believe the gospel."

> Passing alongside the Sea of Galilee, he saw Simon and Andrew the brother of Simon casting a net into the sea, for they were fishermen. And Jesus said to them, "Follow me, and I will make you to become fishers of men." And immediately they left their nets and followed him. And going on a little farther, he saw James the son of Zebedee and John his brother, who were in their boat mending the nets. And immediately he called them, and they left their father Zebedee in the boat with the hired servants and followed him.

> And they went into Capernaum, and immediately on the Sabbath he entered the synagogue and was teaching. And they were astonished at his teaching, for he taught them as one who had authority, and not as one of the scribes. And immediately there was in their synagogue a man with an unclean spirit. And he cried out, "What have you to do with us, Jesus of Nazareth? Have you come to destroy us? I know who you are—the Holy One of God." But Jesus rebuked him, saying, "Be silent, and come out of him!" And the unclean spirit, convulsing him and crying out with a loud voice, came out of him. And they were all amazed, so

that they questioned among themselves, saying, "What is this? A new teaching with authority! He commands even the unclean spirits, and they obey him." And at once his fame spread everywhere throughout all the surrounding region of Galilee (Mark 1:14-28).

Mark tells us about something happening in the infancy of the church. This is at the very moment that Jesus is building what the Apostle Paul will call the foundation stones of the church. Paul says Jesus is gifting the church through apostles and evangelists and pastors and teachers; he is calling out these men to be with him and he is driving them, Mark says, *immediately* into a situation that is scary and startling.

The church in its infancy finds itself, with Jesus, in spiritual warfare against dark spiritual forces. Every stage of the church ever since has found itself in spiritual warfare alongside Jesus. When the Apostle Paul says, I would not have you to be children, "tossed to and fro...by every wind of doctrine" (Ephesians 4:14), this is a tumult that begins at the very start of Jesus' mission and ministry. It belongs, Jesus says, now to us as we carry out that mission.

Notice three things here.

THE AUTHORITY OF CHRIST IN HIS TEACHING

After Jesus has assembled His disciples, He walks in to this synagogue in Capernaum. Jesus is standing up and reading the Scriptures. And as He is teaching on the Scriptures, the text tells us the people there are astounded. The language here says they are literally being "taken aback." There are gasps going on in the room. Why are they so shocked and so amazed? Because He is teaching with authority, and He is teaching not as one of the scribes. He is teaching with an authority that is different from what it is that they have heard in the religious leaders around them. "Who is this?" they say to one another. "What is this? What is going on here?"

Jesus himself is personally reading the Old Testament and interpreting the Old Testament. If you walk out of that synagogue and disregard what has been said, you are disregarding Jesus. The exact same thing is going on in every single one of your Sunday school classes and your vacation Bible schools, and your backyard Bible clubs, and your neighborhood outreaches to children. The exact same thing is going on. Jesus treats the Scripture in such a way that it is astounding to people because he holds to the authority of this Scripture. Think of the difference between the way that Jesus speaks about the temple, and the way that He speaks about the Scriptures; or the way that Jesus speaks about the Sabbath, and the way that He speaks about the Scriptures; the way Jesus treats the dietary and food laws, and the way Jesus treats the Scriptures. He is treating the Scriptures with a gravity and an authority that is immediately noticeable to the people who are hearing Him. Why?

When you are teaching and training up children to be people of the Bible, you are teaching them and training them to understand biblical inspiration, "all Scripture is God-breathed." That is exactly what you see happening in embryonic form right here. Peter tells us later on that men of old wrote the Scriptures as they are "carried along by the Holy Spirit." Peter has been carried along by the Holy Spirit from the very beginning of His interactions with Jesus. How does that happen? Jesus speaks, "Come and follow me," and these men drop their nets. This is not the same as leaving your vocation as a physical therapist in order to become a preacher of the Gospel. When they drop their nets, they are abandoning an economic engine for their families that is passed down to them from father to son, a legacy that they were to leave to their own children. When they walk away from the Lake of Galilee, they are walking away not only from their past, but also from their future. Why are they walking away? What is driving them to walk away? Simply because Jesus speaks to them, "Come and follow me."

When we are teaching the Scripture, teaching children to love and revere the Scripture, we are not teaching children to love and revere a thing. We are teaching children to love and to revere a Person. Why does Jesus speak with such authority? It's because when He reads these Old Testament Scriptures and stands up and explains these Old Testament Scriptures, he is expounding upon something He has written and that He continues to empower by His Spirit.

The Apostle Peter tells us that the men of old in the Old Testament are writing the Scriptures, and how are they writing? Through the Spirit of Christ. Jesus doesn't just show up two-thirds of the way into your Bibles. Jesus has been actively working in the breathing out of the Scriptures, and He is the fulfillment and pinnacle point of those Scriptures. So, when we are teaching our children the inspiration and the uniqueness of the Bible, we are showing them something that is true about Jesus.

When we are teaching and training our children to believe in the inerrancy of Scripture—that all of the Scripture is true and we are held accountable to that Scripture—we are teaching them that Jesus is trustworthy in what He says. The Scripture and the Word of God is the voice of Jesus Himself. Jesus says, "I am calling My sheep. I am ruling My sheep. I am tending My sheep." How does He drive His sheep along? He says it is with His voice. The shepherd knows their name, and the shepherd calls out to them, and therefore, He says, "My sheep hear my voice, and they follow after Me." If you are keeping your children away from the Bible, you are keeping your children away from the voice of Jesus Christ.

The people in Capernaum in Mark 1 heard the voice of Jesus Christ. They heard the vibrations coming from his vocal chords, that Northern Galilean accent, yet when you and I come to the text of the Scripture, we are hearing that voice in every bit as true of a sense as those gathered were hearing it in first person. That's the glory of the inspiration and illumination of the Scripture. He is the final authority, and the Bible is what He is speaking to us. That's why holding fast to the Word of Truth is a personal issue.

I don't really mind red letter Bibles; I've got one myself—the words of Jesus in red. I just wish they were honest and printed the whole thing in red, from Genesis 1 to Revelation 22! Because Jesus is speaking in every text of Scripture and one of the first things that we must do in training up children to love the Bible, is to train up children also to love authority.

When Jesus speaks the Word of God, when He explains the Word of God, the people are amazed and they are taken aback by the fact that He is doing so with authority. Why? God has designed—and

God loves—authority and hierarchy because the entire universe is built on a kingship. This isn't raw sovereignty. This is an authority that seeks and saves and loves. But this is a genuine authority. If in your children's ministry, you are tearing down a sense of authority by doing what the external culture is doing in making a fetish out of youth, and making a fetish out of triviality, then how do you expect children to recognize the voice of authority when they hear it?

"I learned," the psalmist says, "to trust you at my mother's breast." The direction of pastors and elders and teachers and lay leaders in having a sense of maturity and gravity in children's ministry is one of foremost importance. You do not need to find volunteers who are the most like the children in order to lead them! Instead, when there is a sense of weightiness and there is a sense of authority, you are pointing children toward their ultimate allegiance to the authority that is found in Scripture. You are not a peer with the children. You are not a buddy with the children. You are instead a leader and a teacher, and you are pointing and driving them along to maturity and to recognize authority. When the children see servant leadership—as you lead and teach and instruct and rebuke—as being good and being right, they recognize something that is true about the universe itself. When they read the Scriptures and they hear the Scriptures, they are hearing a personal authority. This is exactly what is amazing the people in Capernaum in Mark 1, and it amazes people right now to this day.

Jesus is announcing the Kingdom of God. He is announcing, "Believe the Gospel of God." Jesus is calling these disciples simply with His Word, and Jesus is speaking the Word in a way that creates a tumult. What is happening here is exactly what we see later on when Jesus speaks to the wind and the waves, and they're silent. "Who is this that He is able to speak like this?"

Jesus has an authority that shows up even in the way that He names. When I meet someone for the first time, I'm going to ask her where she's from, what she's doing, ask about her ministry. I am not going to say to her, "Hey Tina, it was great to meet you, but I want you to know; your new name is Sharon." Her response would be, "Who do you think you are?"

Jesus, though, is consistently changing names. "Simon, son of John, I say to you, you are Peter." "Abram, I say to you that you are Abraham." "Sarai, I say to you that you are Sarah." And in every one of those instances, what Jesus is speaking seems to be absurd. Abram is not the father of many nations; he's not the father of anybody! Jacob, renamed Israel, is not one who has wrestled with God and won; he is walking away with a limp. He barely survived! And Simon does not look at all like a rock! What is Jesus doing? He declares something to be true, and then He makes it true. Abram becomes a father of many nations. Israel becomes the vehicle for the blessing of the nations of the world. Simon Peter becomes one of those 12 foundation stones in the new Jerusalem that comes down. Scripture says that there is a new name that Jesus is giving to all of His people, a name that you do not yet know, that you will receive written on a white stone, a name that would seem ridiculous to you right now, but that is who Jesus is making you into. He declares it to be true, and then He makes it to be true.

When you are teaching and training your children, a sense of the weight and authority of the Bible ought to be seen, even in the way that we read the text. We must actually read the text and not simply paraphrase stories of the text. Children need to hear the *words* of God because when they hear the *words* of God, they are not just hearing a story, they are not just hearing doctrines, they are hearing Jesus Christ. That voice, that light, that is how we come to know Jesus. When Saul of Tarsus is turned around, he is turned around by a light and by a voice. "Saul, Saul. Why are you persecuting me?"

You and I have heard that same voice, and with it comes the authority of Jesus that comes through the teaching, and the preaching, and the reading, and the praying through the Bible.

AN AUTHORITY IN THE SPIRIT WORLD

As Jesus is teaching in the synagogue, Scripture tells us there is a man who stands up and screams out. There is an unclean, evil spirit in him, and he cries out, "What do you have to do with us, Jesus of Nazareth? We know who you are, the Holy One of God." This is not an aberration; the Word is being proclaimed. The voice of Jesus is being heard, and when the voice of Jesus is heard, the unclean spirits that wish to exult themselves against the name of Christ are stirred into activity. That's exactly why the Apostle Paul—when he says Jesus has given us the gift of apostles and prophets and evangelists and teachers that He is building his church on—says, "and you will have those come among you through craftiness and through cunning, seeking to have you disturbed and tossed, like children to and fro with every wind of doctrine."

If you are going to have a children's ministry that is rooted and grounded in the Gospel and the Kingdom, you must understand the dark forces that will come against the truth of God—that will be incited and summoned by the teaching, preaching, instruction, and discipleship from the Word of God. When Jesus is telling the Parable of the Sower and the Soils, He says that one of the seeds is snatched away. That is a personal activity from these unclean beings. In order for children to hear and understand the Gospel, to be raised up toward maturity, we do not need to hide from them the dark aspects that the Scripture tells us about. They already know that something is wrong in the universe. That's the reason why every little boy in America loves Maurice Sendak's *Where the Wild Things Are.* He knows something wild is out there and there's something wild inside him, and this little boy speaks to those wild things and with a word, he becomes the king of all the wild things, and they are tamed. What's inside him is tamed, what's outside of him is tamed. If only it were so easy!

That wildness doesn't end. It goes from the temper tantrums of the 3-year-old, to the hormonal surges of puberty, to the identity crises of the teenage years, to the midlife crises of adulthood, to the sense of loneliness, anxiety, and fear lying in a nursing home bed as your memory is fading away. Those aspects of wildness and darkness, they remain, and if we are going to lead children toward Jesus, we must teach the whole counsel of God, which includes showing them the heroic, adventurous sense of Scripture in which Jesus, through His blood on the cross, has silenced the accusations of the evil spirits.

The reason that Jesus is able to stand here and speak to this man is because Jesus says later, "the ruler of this world is coming; he has no claim on me." Every other son of Adam and every other daughter of Eve who has stood before the devil has heard, "I know who you are. I know what you've done. You belong with me in the lake of fire, and here is why..." And in every other instance, the accusation is true. But Jesus says, "He has no claim on me."

Your children already have an imagination that is moving them toward a sense of adventure and a sense of the conquering of the dark forces in the universe. The question is not whether your children in your churches will have that sense. The question is whether you will direct that toward the teaching of the Scripture or allow it to be redirected toward zombies and vampires and video games. Will you direct them to the Scriptures that say, "Yes, everything that you fear about the universe is true and even more so, but Jesus is triumphant through the Gospel," or not?

Right now, in your children's ministry, no matter what it is, you are doing spiritual warfare in the heavenly places—not only as the evil spirits come forward to subvert what you are teaching to the children, but also because in order to teach and disciple children and adults, you have to discern "where am I subverting the teaching of the Scriptures?" The only way that I am able to preach the Bible, and teach my children the Bible at home at night, is to recognize: *I don't believe the Bible.* I'm a liberal. Not in my theory, not in my doctrine, but so often in my heart. I found myself one time reading the Sermon on the Mount, when there was a situation going on in my life, and I read the Sermon on the Mount exactly the way a feminist would read 1 Timothy 2, "Well, it can't mean that, so it must mean something else!" Why? For the exact same reasons. There is something in my heart that I am protecting, and the Word of Jesus that comes through the teaching of the whole counsel of God pierces, slices, and cuts through this and it disturbs these evil forces who cry out, "We know who you are. We know what you're here for." With the Word, with the Bible, Jesus is able to drive this back and to march on victorious, including in your children's ministry.

AN AUTHORITY THAT IS IN HIMSELF

When Jesus walks out of that synagogue, the people are saying not only, "Look at this authority. Can you believe what happened here?"

They're saying to themselves, "Who is this? What is this? Why are these things happening to us?" That is what happens anytime the authority of Christ, found in the inspired and inerrant, clear and sufficient Scriptures is taught. Everything in the Scriptures is pointing toward Christ and is pointing toward the Gospel. As you are reading and taking your children through these Old Testament texts, the Bible is giving you pictures ahead of time of Jesus Christ. Then the Bible is showing you, in every instance, how this person in the Old Testament stories is *not* Jesus Christ. David is anointed with the Spirit of God. He is announced to be the king, the son of God. He is sent out with the Spirit to defeat the enemies of God. He is ruling over the people of God. But by the time you get to 1 Kings 1, he is shivering in the bed, unable even to lift his head up from the pillow. Solomon is wise and all things are put under his feet. He is able to rule God's people with words of wisdom, and yet Solomon ends up losing his kingdom as it splits apart beneath him. He is *like* Christ. He is not Christ.

Here is what you should be looking for: *and here is the one who is yet to come.* Your children already understand this. If you don't think they understand it, try reading C. S. Lewis's *Chronicles of Narnia* to them. An atheist skeptic Laura Miller wrote a book about Narnia. She talks about how, as a child, she loved the *Chronicles of Narnia,* and then there came a point where, after she was grown, she found out that Lewis was a Christian, and she started finding out what all these things were about, and she was enraged by it. But she said, "I loved Aslan."

Your children are able to see, even in that fictional story, a picture of what it means to be Christ. When you are teaching and preaching the Bible, that Jesus Himself has breathed out, you are not stopping with the pictures. You are not stopping with the principles. You are moving to Jesus, and Him crucified. The way, often, that we teach the Bible and never get to Jesus Christ, is exactly the way that the devil is preaching to Jesus in the wilderness temptations. The devil comes to Jesus with Scripture. He quotes Scriptures to Jesus that are, for the most part, true. But they are abstracted from the Gospel. "Turn these stones into bread." Is it good for Jesus to eat bread? Yes! God gives us "daily bread." Sit down and eat bread with us in the Kingdom of God.

But Satan says, "Eat it now." Make yourself a sinner just as Adam was so that you cannot be the redeemer of the world.

Is it good for Jesus to be seen publicly, to be vindicated by God? Yes, and that's what happens at the resurrection from the dead! But the devil quotes to Him the Psalm, "'God will not let you have even your foot dash up against a stone.' Throw yourself from the pinnacle of the temple." Do it now, not at the resurrection from the dead, do it without the cross.

Is it good for Jesus to have all of the kingdoms of the world? Yes! And that is where the biblical story ends—the kingdoms of this world have become the Kingdom of our God and of His Christ, and He will reign forever and ever. Satan says, "all authority over these things has been given to me."—That's true; the whole world lies under the sway of the Wicked One (1 John 5). Satan says, "I will give it to you, if you will just bow down to me." Satan is willing to have a world that Jesus is ruling, a world in which there is no abortion, no pornography, no drunkenness, no domestic violence, no genocide, no disobedience to parents—as long as there is not a cross. As long as there is not the Gospel.

The prosperity gospel teachers who are going all around the world right now are preaching the Bible—many of them are preaching intricately from the book of Deuteronomy—but what are they doing? They are using the text of Deuteronomy, bypassing Jesus, and going straight to you. "You will be blessed if you are obedient. You will be cursed if you are disobedient." Rather than seeing those promises hidden in the obedient Christ who was cursed for us and who was raised for us, they apply it to having a Bentley, or being saved out of unemployment, or having cancer cells removed from your body and heart tissue healthy again. They bypass Jesus, and often that is exactly what we do in the way that we are teaching our children. Jesus had friends—you have friends. David was brave—you be brave. Solomon was wise—you be wise. All of that is true, but none of it makes sense unless it is fitted in the overall picture of the Bible, in which the voice of Jesus consistently speaking in all 66 books, says "All of these prophets, sages, and apostles, they are all pointing to me." Which means children's ministry has to be teaching the cross.

There's another extreme that I want to warn us against. We as evangelicals often have the temptation to simply run from one bogey-man to another. We're afraid of this, so we run over there to that. Sometimes there are people who are afraid, rightly, of the kind of Christless moralism that we have had so often in our churches, especially in children's ministry. They want to run instead to say, "Teach the indicatives—who you are in Christ—not the imperatives—what it is that you are to do." Jesus makes no such distinction. If you see who you are in Christ, that means you listen to the voice of Christ, you are growing up into the head (Ephesians 4), and the head controls the movements of the body. The sheep are following after the Shepherd, and how are they following? Through His voice. Abraham is faithful when he offers up Isaac because he believed that God was able to raise him from the dead. Just as the Pharisees put a hedge around the law so that they wouldn't have to worry about violating it, we can put a hedge around the Gospel and say, "In order to protect ourselves from legalism, we are going to so emphasize who we are in Christ, that we will never speak of what it is that Jesus commands." Or, when we do speak of what Jesus commands, it is so muted and so tamed that it doesn't carry the scary force of what Jesus says. That is not the voice of Jesus Christ.

Jesus' fame spread throughout all of Galilee, and that fame was disruptive. If your children's ministry is anchored in the inspired, inerrant, clear, sufficient Word of God, you're going to find your idolatries being plucked up, the inciting of the evil spirits, and you're going to have the offense of the cross. Blood spattering is not just scary to kids. The crucifixion is not just disturbing to kids. It is disturbing to Simon Peter who confessed, "I believe you are the Christ, the Son of God." Peter saw how all of the prophets and Elijah and John the Baptist are flowing toward Jesus. But when Jesus said, "the Son of Man must be arrested and beaten and crucified," he said, "Lord, never will this happen to you. I will fight for you." Jesus calls that response satanic.

You can train your children to be Satanists even with the Bible as long as you do not drive them in every single text, command, promise, warning, song of rejoicing, and poem of lament to Jesus Christ. The fact is, there was a hole in the ground in the Middle East in which there was a corpse, but sometime before dawn on some Sunday morning, an eyelid crusted over with blood, opened. Cold, dead heart tissue started to beat again. A spike-torn hand started to twitch. As that body stood up and pulled off that face cloth and wrapped it up and laid it on the grave where He had been as a corpse, God was announcing, "This is my beloved Son in whom I am well pleased." Since we are in Christ, God has already announced that to us, about us: "You are my beloved child, in whom I am well pleased. There is therefore now no condemnation for you." Listen to Him. That brings a kind of enraged tranquility. We are able not to panic as we're raising up children in a difficult age in a difficult culture. But we don't love the difficulties either. You rage against the reptile, and yet you know the triumph that comes through the cross.

The teaching of Christ to children will incite the principalities and powers in many ways and many different fashions. If you will teach the Bible as the Bible is given—as the voice of Jesus that points to Jesus and drives us to Jesus—you will hear opposing voices that will say, "Have you come to destroy us?" Then, with "all authority in heaven and on earth" that Jesus says has been given to Him, and He gives to us—you are able to say back, "Yes, we have. Jesus is Lord."

RUSSELL MOORE is President of the Ethics & Religious Liberty Commission of the Southern Baptist Convention. He and his wife Maria are the parents of five sons.

10

Holding Fast to the Word Under Cultural Pressures

Are we raising Canaanites or believers?

R. ALBERT MOHLER JR.

MY PARENTS TOOK me to church from the very beginning of my life in ways too few children today experience. For a Southern Baptist kid, it was a full-body immersion experience—in both time and space. Which meant I was at church 10 to 15 hours a week. I lived in the age where little boys went to church with clunky big white leather shoes and little overalls with shorts. That was when you got dressed up for Sunday morning. It was a big deal.

One Easter Sunday morning when I was three, I ran up to my pastor and leapt into his arms, and when he picked me up, I planted two big feet of red clay on his white suit...before the sermon. I can still remember that because of the trauma it caused my mother. But I remember him hugging me and setting me down. We need more preachers three-year-old little boys want to run up to, just to be picked up and loved.

PEOPLE OF THE COVENANT, NOT CANAANITES

The Christian church is called to a multigenerational vision, just as Israel was, and we must embrace that vision of our responsibility and our Christian identity.

Deuteronomy 6 includes the seminal verse in the experience of Israel, the *Shema*. Deuteronomy 6:4 says, "Hear O Israel, the LORD thy God, the LORD is one." It is, of course, a statement of monotheism, but it goes beyond that. It is a statement of *covenantal monotheism*; it is addressed to Israel. "Hear O *Israel* the LORD thy God, the LORD is one."

Let's consider what's at stake for Israel as these words are spoken. Deuteronomy includes the last words that we have from Moses—what he was assigned to preach as God prepared the children of Israel for entry into the land of promise. As you'll recall, Moses was not going to lead them into the land of promise. Rather, he would die on the brink of Israel's acceptance of this promise.

In the five massive messages of Deuteronomy, we understand that this is God getting His people ready for entry into the land of promise, but the book also reflects God's servant Moses, in terms of his final testimony to the children of Israel. In view of biblical history, the very fact that they are on the brink of Canaan means that this is a generation that will not remember having lived in Egypt.

As it is in almost every time, there's good news and bad news. The good news is that this generation did not have the bitter memory of having lived under bondage to Pharaoh in Egypt and had not experienced the lash of Pharaoh's taskmasters. They had not experienced the bitterness of that life in which Pharaoh sought to kill them. They did not have direct memory of when Pharaoh ordered the Hebrew midwives to kill the Hebrew boys immediately after they were born. After the midwives sidestepped Pharaoh's mandate, he ordered the massacre of the little boys of the children of Israel. They wouldn't have remembered that, and that's good news. But it's also the bad news: they didn't remember this.

This is the problem reflected in Deuteronomy chapter 6. You will notice the language about "sons." There is generational concern that is encoded into this chapter because the great concern is that these children, who did not know how to be Jews in Egypt, will not know how to be God's covenant people in Canaan.

Those who did not know Pharaoh's bitter lash will be seduced by Canaan's many charms. Suffice it to say, that we must assume the default for babies born in Canaan is that they would end up as Canaanites. You live in Canaan? Guess what, in all likelihood you're going to become a Canaanite.

Which is to say that one of the realities we face in terms of human life, after the fall, is that the culture tends to produce its own. The dominant culture always tends to replicate itself in every successive generation. This is exactly why, in Romans 12, Paul tells the church not to be conformed to the world, but to be transformed by the renewing of the mind. This cultural pressure of acculturation and the loss of Christian identity, the loss of covenantal commitment, the loss of the Christian worldview, the loss of children—this is not something new. This is something right out of the experience of the first-century church, and the first-century church would have recognized that as going all the way back to Deuteronomy 6.

The default is that if we're going to live in Canaan, our children will be Canaanites, unless there is some massive intervention that will prevent it. The last thing that should surprise us, given the biblical worldview, is that our children will look like the culture around them. That should never surprise us. The exception is anyone who would stand over as separate from that culture.

Now the background of Canaan simply cannot be ignored here. What's going on in Canaan? Why would Canaanite culture be attractive to those who should be the sons and daughters of the covenant of Israel? The Bible is incredibly candid in telling us that the Canaanites were not only idolaters, they were idolaters of power, sex, and material success. And we can trace all of this from what is forbidden to Israel by God's law, specifically telling Israel they may not do what the Canaanites are doing. Canaanism can't be reformed. The Lord says, don't even take their high places and get rid of all the Canaanite religion and create places of worship to me. There has to be an absolute separation. There could be no syncretism, no mixing together of what it means to be a Canaanite and what it means to be a child of the covenant.

Verse 4 is the central verse in Deuteronomy 6. "Hear O Israel, the LORD our God, the LORD is one." This is the verse that every Jewish boy was to learn to read first, before reading anything else. It is the central verse of Israel's identity. But the historical context is in the narrative. "Now this is the commandment—the statutes and the rules— that the Lord your God commanded me to teach you." Moses is here commanded to teach these commandments. Why? That *you*—not I, not we—"that you may be able to do them in the land to which you are going over, to possess it." The summary of it all was found in verse 2, "that you may fear the Lord your God, you and your son and your son's son, by keeping all his statutes and his commandments, which I command you, all the days of your life, and that your days may be long." The covenantal promise was that long days and length of life would be attached to fidelity to the covenant and obedience to the statues and the laws.

This multigenerational vision is what the Christian church is called to, just as Israel was called to it. We're not to be concerned just with our son, but with our son's son, and with our son's son's son, and our daughter's daughter's daughter. We must have a multigenerational vision of our responsibility and of our Christian identity. If we don't, we should not be surprised when those generations become *Canaanites*.

Which is to say that right now we are investing and we are teaching. We are serving as examples for a generation that will, once we are dead, have a great deal to do with whether or not our grandchildren and our great-grandchildren will be Canaanites or not. Moses knew, when he was used of God to give this message, that he would not be able to be with the people when they entered the Land of Promise, much less once there was a generational transfer. And he knew this: If they would follow these commands and statutes they would be the people of the covenant, not Canaanites. He wrote, "Hear O Israel, therefore and be careful to do them." In the Hebrew it's not just *believe* the commandments, it's not just *obey* the commandments, consistently, it's *do* them. This is what we're called to *do*. In the Hebrew understanding, doing and being were so closely united that you be them, you do them, you are them.

"Hear, O Israel: The Lord your God, the Lord is one. You shall love the Lord your God with all your heart and with all your soul and with all your might." Once again, this is the central verse of Israel. When the Pharisees and the Sadducees got into a debate and went to Jesus, and the Pharisees asked Jesus, "what then is the greatest commandment?" They were not surprised when Jesus said the greatest commandment is that you are to love the Lord your God with all your heart, and soul, and *mind*.

What surprised them is that he went to an obscure verse in Leviticus and then went on to say, "And a second is like it: You shall love your neighbor as yourself. All the Law and the Prophets hang on these two commandments." So the Law and the Prophets, the entirety of the old covenant, is hanging on this verse, "You shall love the Lord your God with all your heart and with all your soul and with all your might."

DOCTRINE

Three words leap out from Deuteronomy 6: *doctrine, discipline,* and *diligence.*

The first word to see is *doctrine.* What we learn from this passage, in terms of what it means to *teach* and to *contend for* is that it is inescapably theological. It's unapologetically doctrinal. The core of doctrine simply means teaching, and here you have the order to teach. The children of Israel will not be expected to know what they were not taught, and they can't possibly live what they do not know. Here you have the logic of Scripture made very clear. "You shall teach them diligently to your children, and shall talk of them when you sit in your house, and when you walk by the way" (v. 7). The teaching here is absolutely central, and the teaching has content. Notice, as you see, in verse 10, we're not talking about some vague, abstract deity who is perhaps generic and could be applied to different religious systems. Rather, this is the God of Abraham, Isaac, and Jacob.

Verse 13 says, "It is the Lord your God you shall fear. Him you shall serve and by his name you shall swear." The warning is here, "You shall not go after other gods, the gods of the peoples who are around you—for the Lord your God in your midst is a jealous God—lest the anger of the Lord your God be kindled against you, and he destroy you from off the face of the earth." It requires teaching, and the teaching requires specific doctrine. The Israelites cannot possibly be expected to know the God of Israel unless they are taught of the God of Israel. They cannot possibly expect to live according to His commandments and His statutes unless they are taught them. Teaching requires this intentional, perhaps even monomaniacal, focus on the part of parents and those who work with children, and of the church in general, to teach, and to teach, and to teach.

It's not just the action of teaching; It's the content of the doctrine that is taught. If we're going to contend for the whole counsel of God, then we're going to have to teach it. But of course, that means before you teach it, you have to know it. I believe that complementarity between men and women, in the home and in the church, is a central issue, not only of faithfulness but also of the display of God's glory, for one very important reason. If dad's going to teach this, he's got to study it.

I think God's glory is in that—in a father having to study in order to teach. If a dad knows he is going to have to teach, then he is going to have to study and know. And in teaching, he will lead. Here you have the very same principle. Israel will only be faithful if its fathers teach. Of course, this is in some sense extended to all parents, but it's not an accident that in this divine revelation, it's a specific assignment to fathers to teach. And the content is made very clear. It is the content of God's Word, His Law.

You'll also notice that something else becomes very crucial in terms of how this teaching is to take place. One of the most powerful demonstrations of how we teach the Gospel is by narrative. And the saving narrative of God is where God directed Moses to instruct the children of Israel, as seen in verse 20 and following: "When your son asks you in time to come, 'What is the meaning of the testimonies and the statutes and the rules that the Lord our God has commanded you?'"

You'll notice here that Israel's fathers are not told that they are merely to say, "We do all these things because God said so." Would that be enough? Of course it would be enough in terms of authority, but it's not enough in terms of understanding.

God himself said,

> When your son asks you in time to come, "What is the meaning of the testimonies and the statutes and the rules that the Lord our God has commanded you?' then you shall say to your son, 'We were Pharaoh's slaves in Egypt. And the Lord brought us out of Egypt with a mighty hand. And the Lord showed signs and wonders, great and grievous, against Egypt and against Pharaoh and all his household, before our eyes. And he brought us out from there, that he might bring us in and give us the land that he swore to give to our fathers. And the Lord [that is the same Lord who did these things, who brought us out of captivity to Pharaoh in Egypt, the same God who showed us signs and wonders, great and grievous, this same Lord] commanded us to do all these statutes, to fear the Lord our God, for our good always, that he might preserve us alive...(Deuteronomy 6:20-24a).

That's an amazing statement. Just imagine Israel's story—what a story Israel got to tell. *We were once slaves to Pharaoh in Egypt.*

What about us? When our children say, "Why do we live this way? Why do we live according to these rules? Why do we believe these things? Why are we bound by the authority of Scripture? Why must we live this way?" Then you shall say to your son, "We were once slaves to sin. We were under bondage to sin."

We've got to continually raise our children not to be Canaanites, and we've got to be grounding them in a story in which they understand that what it means to be a Christian—and what we hope and pray it will mean for them individually when they come to faith in Christ—is that they will be delivered from the domain of darkness and transferred into "the kingdom of his beloved Son, in whom we have redemption, the forgiveness of sins" (Colossians 1:13-14).

That's a story. It's not that we look back to Exodus and say, "Well, the cross was fulfilled in Exodus." No, we look at the cross and the resurrection of our Lord Jesus Christ—the saving work of Christ, the atonement accomplished by Christ—and we say, "It's that to which Exodus was pointing." The Exodus is the lesser, and the cross is the infinitely greater. We're going to have to teach the whole counsel of

God. We're going to need to ground our children in Scripture. We're going to have to make sure they find themselves in the storyline of Scripture. We're going to have to make sure that they grow from being infants to toddlers to children, and into adolescents, knowing themselves in that story. Otherwise, they're going to be in some other story.

This also means we have to confront them with their own identity as a sinner and present to them the Gospel as the good news of salvation that comes to all who believe and repent of their sins, in such a way that they not only know that's our story, but it becomes their story, and they come to faith in Christ.

That's why we need to help our children understand how conversion is such a great gift and miracle of God, such that this story, writ at the individual level, is the same because this is my story. I wasn't a slave to Pharaoh in Egypt, but I was a slave to sin. But Jesus saved me. He brought me out by His mighty arm and His outstretched hand through all that was accomplished for me by Christ.

DISCIPLINE

The second word is "discipline." You will notice the moral discipline, the life that is required of God's covenant people. You would know who they are by how they live in Canaan. If they lived as Canaanites, you would have no way to distinguish them from anyone else. But they don't live as Canaanites; they live according to the discipline of God.

It is a word that is used over and over and over again. Of course, we can't escape the word "teaching" but it is that teaching that is applied in terms of how Israel was to live. You'll notice the moral exhortations that are so clear in this passage, and as you see in the entirety of God's law, especially in the first five books of the Bible, what Israel is to do and what Israel is not to do. "Hear therefore, O Israel, and be careful to do them," that is, the commandments, "that it may go well with you." When you get to the end of the book of Deuteronomy, the Lord will say through Moses, "See, I have set before you life and death, blessing and curse. Choose life and live." The commandments are inescapably moral.

When I was a child, my parents did not have, nor did they necessarily at that time need, the understanding that they were throwing me to the enemy every time I walked out the front door. It's different now. My point is not to lament something that is past. Again, in every age there is blessing and there is curse. We have a unique opportunity to be faithful in the present, in order that our children and grandchildren and great-grandchildren may be faithful in the future. We need to understand our children are being thrown to the enemy. You can call the enemy Hollywood, the entertainment industrial complex, the intellectual elites, the tenured faculty at your local university. You can look at the cultural authorities; this is how culture works.

In Canaan, the culture worked because it was a pervasive system of beliefs, moral teaching, entertainment, avocation, economics, and politics that all coalesced around the worship of these deities, these idols.

Even though you can look back at that and say it was a crude culture, our culture is trending there. Every culture is a system of beliefs and intellectual principles and moral reflexes and emotional responses and entertainment and economics and politics, and all the things that make society work around us, and make the world make sense to the people who live around us. There was a time when a nominal Christianity so shaped this culture that you couldn't tell, necessarily, who was a Christian and who wasn't because in order to be considered upright and esteemed by society, at least in terms of some identifiable moral issues, you had to live like a Christian, even if you weren't a Christian.

But that world is entirely gone. We're not looking back at a golden era that has passed with lament. But in terms of many issues, right on the front lines of where we're living right now, I was not being thrown to the enemy when I was sent to school; it was basically the same message. I wasn't being thrown to the enemy when I went to the Boy Scouts; it was essentially the same message. I wasn't being thrown to the enemy, and the enemy wasn't necessarily looking for me the same way that the culture is working now. When you look at this, you come to understand that we are facing a situation in which our children are going to be Canaanites unless there is a massive effort to ground them. When people say, "If you don't stop this teaching, your children—college-aged children, young adults—they're going to leave." I simply have to say, "I think, according to Scripture, this means we've got to teach it more."

Because it's going to have to be grounded in them, not merely as something that we believe, but as something that they deeply believe. They're going to have to understand at some point that the Gospel is clearly at stake, and so are their children and their children's children.

Here you see the discipline that is required. It is so clear, and the stakes are set so clearly in Scripture, too. "You shall not put the LORD your God to the test, as you tested him at Massah. You shall diligently keep the commandments of the LORD your God...And you shall do what is right and good in the sight of the LORD, that it may go well with you" (Deuteronomy 6:16-18).

I think this is one of the greatest things a parent can say to a child: "You see, you need to do this, so things will go well with you and you'll live long. I want you to know what going well for you looks like, and I'm going to have to make clear what not going well looks like. And if you want things to go well with you, this is what you're going to do—you're going to obey the Lord your God."

DILIGENCE

The last word in this is Look at verse 7, "You shall teach them diligently to your children, and shall talk of them when you sit in your house, and when you walk by the way, and when you lie down, and when you rise." In other words, all the time. What are you to be doing? Teaching your children. Every opportunity is an opportunity to teach.

You're teaching all the time whether you know it or not. You're teaching, we might say, effectively or ineffectively, but you're always teaching. Whenever we are before a child, in the vision of a child, the child is learning. Here we are told that in addressing ourselves to the children of the covenant—addressed here to the covenant children of Israel—and then to the children who are given to Christian parents in the Christian home, and the ministry of the Christian church, there is a diligence that is required.

Let me go back to the hours I spent at church—10 to 15 hours a week. Let me ask, how many hours of any kind of Christian instruction or any kind of explicit Christian intentional experience do children, and young people, and teenagers receive today? In a given week, how much of the child's time do you have? This points to one of the problems. As any teacher knows, students are only learning a percentage of the time what we want to teach.

Parents need to invest more of their time with their children, and quality time. Guess what quality time is? Time! Now, I understand, you want more undistracted time and more time with intentionality, but the fact is, it's still time.

It's diligence that is required because you're going to have to go over it over and over and over again because they don't retain very well. Nor do you, by the way. The reason why you may know more than you would otherwise know is because you're teaching them.

The Wall Street Journal came out with a news story in which children said their parents stopped reading to them aloud too early. Eighty percent of the children surveyed said they wished their parents would still sometimes read aloud to them. After I talked about this story on *The Briefing*, I had a dad come up to me and say, "We're reading to our children every day, and we've got a two-year-old, a three-year-old, a six-year-old, an eight-year-old, and a 14-year-old. Everybody has a bath, everybody gets ready, and we tell the four little ones, 'it's time for a bedtime story.'" He added, "You know, that 14-year-old always comes." There's something sweet about that. Just realize, diligence means you want them to hear and you want them to overhear. You take every opportunity to exercise your responsibility as parents and as Christian teachers to teach and be diligent.

It's going to take doctrine. It's going to take discipline. It's going to take diligence. It's going to take each of these to hold fast to the whole counsel of God under cultural pressure to conform. Consider these three challenges in raising the next generation: "Holding Fast," "Whole Counsel of God" and "Cultural Pressures to Conform." Let's work backwards, beginning with the Cultural Pressures to Conform."

CULTURAL PRESSURE TO CONFORM

This just isn't as new as we think. Many evangelicals want to think it's new today. All of a sudden a lot of evangelical churches and parents think we now have to break glass because we face an emergency. Guess what? Go back to Canaan. All those parents were panicking—how in the world are we going to be faithful in this? Well, how in the world did a Christian mom send her 15-year-old son through the streets of Rome past public orgies in order to bring back bread? Somehow, Christian parents had to be faithful in Rome, and Israel's parents had to be faithful in Canaan, and now Christian parents have to be faithful in the Rome/Canaan in which we live today.

God is up to this. I'm not saying we're up to this, but God is up to this. That cultural pressure to conform, we have to recognize, however, is so pervasive that most Christians, even though they exaggerate the newness of this, underestimate the urgency of it. It's a vortex into which we are all being pulled. The cultural pressure to conform is not a symptom of America, uniquely, in our time. It's a symptom of the cosmos inhabited by human beings after Genesis 3.

WHOLE COUNSEL OF GOD

This goes back to Acts 20:27. The problem for many is the word *God*— the fact that there is a God. If there is a God, then what He says is binding. I love the way B. B. Warfield put it in his little book, *The Plan of Salvation*, when he said, "If there is a God, He's God." If you actually believe there is a God, you better sit down and think about what you actually believe. It's the whole counsel of *God*. If there is a God, He is God, and that changes everything.

The word "whole" is another problem here. Nobody is upset with the golden rule. You'll even notice liberal impulses in Christianity with people saying, "I want to be a Red Letter Christian." Whoever says that needs to go and read "the red letters" because Jesus had more to say about hell than about heaven. Jesus preached the love of God in terms of demonstrating it in his teaching and fleshing it out, and of course showing what love means in "while we were still sinners, Christ died for us" (Romans 5:8). Look at the Sermon on the Mount where Jesus said, "you've heard it said..." He didn't take anything back, but He said, "I say unto you," and He took it right to the heart. It's the word "whole" that's a big problem here because we have to understand that where the culture has the biggest problem is where our children are most vulnerable.

Our society is going at anything that suggests that there is one God, one Gospel, one Savior. Just imagine what fortitude it's going to take for children to hold to the Gospel of Jesus Christ in light of the understanding that we really do believe we are accountable to Scripture. In many ways that's the most revolutionary, the most incendiary Christian belief that is at stake right now—the fact we actually believe that we are bound by Scripture.

At the Diet of Worms, Martin Luther said, "Here I stand, I can do none other. God help me. My conscience is bound by Scripture." The very fact we believe we are bound by Scripture is increasingly going to be a public scandal. This is the thing: Unless our children develop a love for the Word of God, and unless the Word of God gets into their hearts and penetrates them, then they're going to see the Word of God as the problem. They're going to see us as the problem for, in their view, basing prejudicial, hateful, exclusionary beliefs upon an inscripturated claim to revelation.

HOLDING FAST

We sang "He Will Hold Me Fast" at church recently. After hearing all these young 20-something voices filling the room with that song during the service, Mary and I got into the car and were talking about the fact that this is a generation that is hanging on the fact that "He will hold me fast." They're not just thinking eschatologically. They're thinking Monday morning in school. They're thinking all week long in the workplace. They're thinking as they go home and put their children to bed, "He will hold me fast."

But there's also a command that we hold fast to the faith. The holding fast is actually something that we are assigned. And holding fast under these cultural conditions, well, let's be honest, it's going to require skills that we weren't required to develop before. It's going to require a sense of intentionality that our parents perhaps didn't have to have with us. It's going to require cultural skills, apologetic skills, doctrinal skills, and theological skills. It's going to require emotional skills, parenting skills, and teaching skills that maybe previous generations didn't need in the same measure and the same proportion, but we need it all now.

That's why I'm so thankful that in local churches there are opportunities right now, perhaps even richer and more Gospel-centered opportunities than were afforded to me when I had those clunky white shoes on and that crazy little pair of shorts with the overalls.

Now I think every moment I spent surrounded by godly people, every moment I heard the Bible taught, every moment I overheard the Bible taught, every time a godly Christian adult spoke to me with respect and loved me, every time I was encouraged in the nurture and admonition of the Lord, I needed it. If I needed it, what will your grandchildren need?

Don't spend time lamenting what we believe has been lost. Remember there's a land of promise to which we are called. Getting safely there, well, for those who are in Christ—Christ will hold us fast.

But when we look at our children and our grandchildren and the church's children, when we look at any child, let's pray that they see Christ, and seeing Christ, believe in Him, and believing, they are saved. Let's pray that they'll be raised in the nurture and admonition of the Lord. Let's hold them fast and hold them close.

R. ALBERT MOHLER JR. is President of The Southern Baptist Theological Seminary. He is married to Mary and they have two grown children, and one grandchild.

Afterword

*The Fruit of Proclaiming the Glorious
Gospel to the Next Generations*

THERE IS A MARVELOUS vision expressed in Psalm 78:1-7. It serves as a calling upon the life of every Christian—every parent, grandparent, teacher, pastor, nursery worker, and church member.

> Give ear, O my people, to my teaching;
> incline your ears to the words of my mouth!
> I will open my mouth in a parable;
> I will utter dark sayings from of old,
> things that we have heard and known,
> that our fathers have told us.
> We will not hide them from their children,
> but tell to the coming generation
> the glorious deeds of the LORD, and his might,
> and the wonders that he has done.
> He established a testimony in Jacob
> and appointed a law in Israel,
> which he commanded our fathers
> to teach to their children,
> that the next generation might know them,
> the children yet unborn,
> and arise and tell them to their children,
> so that they should set their hope in God
> and not forget the works of God,
> but keep his commandments;

We hope and pray that the preceding chapters have given you a renewed and whole-hearted desire to make known to the next generations the majestic glories of our Lord so that our children might set their hope in Jesus alone. We do not always fully see the spiritual fruit of our endeavors in this lifetime, but we can be confident in the sovereign grace of God to accomplish His saving work in the lives of His people. When His Word goes out, it never fails to bring about His purposes. That seemingly bored little girl you teach week-by-week in Sunday school class may, by God grace, become a great woman of faith who dedicates her life to nurturing her family and sharing the Gospel with other women. That rebellious young boy in your own home may, by God's grace, become a man of God who faithfully shepherds a small local church. And often it is through "ordinary" means that God brings about extraordinary fruit in the lives of children—means such as teaching children to read the Bible, memorize Scripture, pray, participate in the worship service, and to observe God's hand in nature.

Consider for a moment this short testimony,

I remember reading my King James Version Bible, from age 6 or 7 every night. It was a habit I got from my parents, and my grandmother encouraged in me as well. I didn't understand everything in it. I could follow along and make out some of the words. It was God's Word and it was fascinating to me. I deeply treasured those words of God from a very early age.

I remember when I was 12, praying one night with my mother to trust Jesus, ask Him into my heart, have Him be my Savior. I made a profession of faith and then was baptized at First Baptist Church in Eau Claire, Wisconsin. I remember coming to Minneapolis at 13 for a Billy Graham Crusade—that would have been 1961—and going forward then as a recommitment of my life. I remember those things but now, looking back earlier in my life, I would not date my conversion to age 12 or 13 because I see evidences of regeneration—genuine saving faith—much, much earlier. I loved to sit at the piano and sing hymns. I loved to read my Bible. When I was out on the playground, riding my bike, or out playing baseball, I would be praying to God quietly during the day. I see evidences way back at a very early stage because of Christian parents who brought me up in a Christian home and brought me to Sunday school, and I'm so thankful for that heritage.

In some ways, this is a very simple, "unspectacular" testimony. A young boy brought to faith through very ordinary means: reading the Bible, encouragement from family, the teaching and preaching of the Word, praying, and singing hymns. Yet, God was pleased to do extraordinary things by His sovereign grace in this young boy's life. Who is the man sharing this testimony? Dr. Wayne Grudem: theologian, author, seminary professor, and defender of the Christian faith. He gave this short testimony during his address, "Teaching the Richness of the Entire Gospel," at our 2007 National Conference.[1] His testimony reflects the importance of the calling laid forth in Psalm 78:1-7. Charles Spurgeon wrote the following concerning those verses:

> We will look forward to future generations, and endeavor to provide for their godly education. It is the duty of the church of God to maintain, in fullest vigor, every agency intended for the religious education of the young; to them we must look for the church of the future, and as we sow towards them so shall we reap.[2]

Godly men and women faithfully sowed the Gospel into the life of Wayne Grudem at a very young age. They did not hide from him "the glorious deeds of the LORD, and his might, and the wonders that he has done." We, and our children, are now reaping some of the rich benefits from that sowing, including three of Dr. Grudem's books: *Systematic Theology: An Introduction to Biblical Doctrine; Bible Doctrine: Essential Teachings of the Christian Faith;* and *Christian Beliefs: Twenty Basics Every Christian Should Know.*

On a very personal note, we at Truth78 have been abundantly blessed by these books. They have taught us to think deeply and

---

[1] Available at Truth78.org/anthology
[2] Charles Haddon Spurgeon, *The Treasury of David,* vol. III (New York, NY: Funk & Wagnalls, 1886), 433.

biblically about the essence and importance of sound doctrine. Dr. Grudem's gift of taking difficult truths and making them understandable for the "average" Christian has inspired and challenged us as we think of ways to teach these truths to children. A seemingly small seed planted in the life of one small boy, in one generation, is now reaping a harvest in the lives of innumerable people in this generation. What a priceless gift from God. This is one more evidence of His glorious deeds; another reason to set our hope in God through Christ! Will you heed the call to continue this great work our Lord has given us? Do you long for the next generations, including your children, to be part of the myriads and myriads in Revelation 5:12-13 who say with a loud voice,

> "Worthy is the Lamb who was slain,
>   to receive power and wealth and wisdom and
>   might and honor and glory and blessing!"

> "To him who sits on the throne and to the Lamb
>   be blessing and honor and glory and might
>   forever and ever!"

Scripture Index

Truth78

TRUTH78 is a vision-oriented ministry for the next generations—that they may know, honor, and treasure God, setting their hope in Christ alone, so that they will live as faithful disciples for the glory of God.

Our mission is to nurture the faith of the next generations by equipping the church and home with resources and training that instruct the mind, engage the heart, and influence the will through proclaiming the whole counsel of God.

We are committed to developing resources and training that are God-centered, Bible-saturated, Gospel-focused, Christ-exalting, Spirit-dependent, doctrinally grounded, and discipleship-oriented.

RESOURCES AND TRAINING MATERIALS

Truth78 offers the following categories of resources and training materials:

CURRICULUM

We publish materials designed for formal Bible instruction. The scope and sequence of these materials reflects our commitment to teach children and youth the whole counsel of God over the course of their education. Materials include curricula for Sunday school, Mid-week Bible programs, Backyard Bible Clubs or Vacation Bible School, and Intergenerational studies. Most of these materials can easily be adapted for use in Christian schools and education in the home.

VISION-CASTING AND TRAINING

We offer a wide variety of booklets, video and audio seminars, articles, and other practical training resources that highlight and further expound our vision, mission, and values, as well as our educational philosophy and methodology. Many of these resources are freely distributed through our website. These resources and training serve to assist ministry leaders, volunteers, and parents in implementing Truth78's vision and mission in their churches and homes.

PARENTING AND FAMILY DISCIPLESHIP

We have produced a variety of materials and training designed to help parents disciple their children. These include booklets, video presentations, family devotionals, children's books, articles, and other recommended resources. Furthermore, our curricula include Growing in Faith Together (GIFT) Pages to help parents apply what is taught in the classroom to their child's daily experience in order to nurture their faith.

BIBLE MEMORY

Our Fighter Verses™ Bible memory program is a unique collection of carefully chosen verses to help fight the fight of faith and is designed to encourage churches, families, and individuals in the lifelong practice and love of Bible memory. It is an easy-to-use Bible memory system, which is available in print, on FighterVerses.com, and as an app (IOS and Android in English, Spanish, French, and German). The Fighter Verses app includes review systems, quizzes, songs, a devotional, and other memory helps. For pre-readers, a separate Foundation Verses set uses simple images to help young children memorize 76 key verses.

GUIDE THE NEXT GENERATIONS TO WALK IN THE TRUTH

LEARN

Truth78 offers opportunities to grow in biblical vision, encouragement, and practical applications for ministry to the next generations through extensive training and conference videos, blog articles, and other helpful documents available at Truth78.org. By subscribing to the Truth78 e-newsletter (**Truth78.org/enewsletter**), you will find weekly updates on new articles and resources.